MODERN
SEQUENCE DANCING
FOR ALL

T. A. WHITWORTH
(CHESTERFIELD)

A

First published 1994
by
T. A. Whitworth,
42 Newbold Back Lane, Chesterfield,
Derbyshire, S40 4HQ.

ISBN 0-9501927-3-2

British Library Cataloguing in Publication Data:

Whitworth, Thomas Alan

Modern Sequence Dancing for All

I. Title II. Fuller, Ken

793.33

ISBN 0-9501927-3-2

Printed in Great Britain by:
Higham Press Limited,
Shirland, Alfreton
Derbyshire,
DE55 6BP.

Foreword

We are often asked in our capacity as dance teachers and holiday hosts if we can recommend a book which will help to unravel the mysteries of Sequence and Old-Time dancing to complement our lessons. Most books on sequence dancing merely contain pages of scripts - this book is completely different. Reading it is like taking a breath of fresh air. It is written in an easily understandable way with useful tips on how to remember sequence dances. Technique is comprehensively covered in an interesting manner without it ever becoming boring. In addition to the normal "foot" diagrams, are novel line drawings which certainly make the figure patterns far easier to remember.

The book provides a mine of information not readily available elsewhere, making this a useful and reliable source of reference, both for the beginner and the advanced dancer alike.

We welcome the rare opportunity to introduce a book which we think is long overdue and the greatest compliment we can give is to heartily recommend it.

Jill and George Stidwell
U.K.A.P.T.D., B.A.T.D.

George and Jill Stidwell

After working for 37 years for B.T., George took early retirement in 1989, due to his office relocation, which left him and Jill free to take up a full-time appointment as professional dance leaders. They are qualified teachers of ballroom, sequence, old-time and rock 'n' roll. For the six months of the Winter season they work overseas for a large holiday company. During the Summer they host dancing holidays in the U.K. and also run a sequence club for beginners and the more advanced dancer in their home town. Their main interest is introducing new people into sequence dancing and this has become a successful second career which they both thoroughly enjoy.

Acknowledgements

My thanks are offered to *Mr. W. H. Share* for a critical reading of the text and to many others for support, advice and encouragement.

I am very grateful indeed to *Mrs. Susan Baker* for type-setting a difficult and demanding manuscript and to my friend and neighbour, *Mr. Wilfrid Eaton*, for designing the cover and drawing the various diagrams throughout the manual.

The book is dedicated, above all, to the dance leaders and teachers who have provided opportunities for my wife and I to enjoy ourselves and put dancing theory into practice.

Contributors

KEN FULLER (see Chapter 15) is one of the small band of people in the Manchester area who helped to put modern sequence dancing on the map. Since 1956 he has been Secretary of the Manchester M.C's Club and has organised dances, led off the sequences and helped people where he could. As well as being a writer of many popular sequence dances, he is a dancer of no mean ability. In 1962 he and his then partner, Margaret, took first place in the NASD new dance competition with his Kingston Quickstep. He has recently been awarded the first Certificate of Merit for services to sequence dancing issued by the 'Dancing World' magazine.

WILFRID EATON (Illustrator) is a local musician and artist who paints regularly at St. Ives. He served in No. 3 Commando from 1942 - 1945.

Contents

Author's Preface

This book is designed to answer some of the many questions which spring to the mind of the newcomer to sequence dancing - it provides much information not readily available elsewhere. It adopts a radically different approach to dancing and more experienced dancers may find it of interest. It does not aim so much to teach dancing as to help the work of the dancing teacher by providing material to study away from the dancing sessions. Nevertheless, a series of graded exercises is provided for the beginner, leading up to the performance of a simple sequence dance. A strategy for learning and remembering sequence dances is developed with appropriate examples.

Great emphasis is placed on dancing figures as an aid to understanding and memorising the sequences. The figures are classified by foot movements rather than by individual dances - this seems particularly suited to the needs of sequence dancers. Figures are related to one another as far as possible and their uses illustrated by reference to various sequence dances. Latin-American and Old-Time styles receive some attention since, under the present system, two-thirds of new award-winning dances come from these areas. Dancing technique and related matters are discussed, although it is stressed that lessons from a qualified teacher are essential to reach the higher levels.

Sequence dancing has a long and interesting history and this is described in the introduction. There is also a chapter by Ken Fuller which sets out the development of the modern sequence style in the Manchester area from 1950 - 1965 in some detail.

An attempt has been made to distil from the wisdom of the past (and present) those elements which are of most direct value to the modern sequence dancer - we hope it has been successful!

To my wife, Margaret, with love and   **T. A. WHITWORTH**
to our children, Margaret Anne,   **January 1994**
Simon, Frances and Brendan.   **A. M. D. G.**

CHAPTER 1

AN INTRODUCTION TO MODERN SEQUENCE DANCING

Essential Features

Have you ever thought that you would like some low-cost healthy activity which would take you out several nights a week to meet friends? Modern sequence dancing might be the answer for you - it is the social phenomenon of the post-war years. Some couples have been sequence dancing for 20 years or more anywhere between 3 and 7 nights per week (with occasional afternoon dances and dancing holidays!).

Despite its popularity sequence dancing is little-known to the general public - it is rarely advertised or seen on TV. It is very much the case that those in the know, know where to go! In many areas there may be 3 or 4 sessions to choose from each evening within easy travelling distance. A typical sequence dancing session is held in a community centre, club, school or church hall to recorded music. The dance leader announces the name of the sequence dance and then leads off with his partner. After 1 or 2 sequences the majority join in - people go to dance - it is not a spectator sport! Some 15 to 20 sequence dances will be performed in a 2 to 3 hour session with a short interval for refreshments.

Now anything that occupies sane, mature people for so much time must have some challenge and interest. Certainly some effort and commitment is required to become a competent sequence dancer. There are thousands of 16-bar sequences and a good repertoire of these is essential to be at ease in sessions in different locations. Learning, however, is not as difficult as it may appear. Sequence dancers are reasonably fit and well-organised but they are not all mental giants or people with great inherent skill. They have started off in most cases like everyone else and made their way up the ladder.

Attending the first sequence dance is a humbling experience for the beginner. Everyone seems to do dances like the Broadway Quickstep, Together Saunter, Tango Serida and anything else that comes up with consummate ease. They go round sometimes talking to one another as though it were as simple as walking. On being shown a new dance many couples can perform it reasonably well after only 2 or 3 demonstrations. This facility comes with practice although some dancers take longer to acquire this skill than others. It is encouraging to hear that many consider that slow learners make the best dancers in the long run. Learning sequence dancing is something like learning to read. How are all the strange shapes of the letters going to be called to mind so that a sentence can be recognised at a glance? Sequence dancing has letters and a language of its own. The instructor may shout out "Reverse Corté", "Back Hover", "Wing", "Open Telemark", etc. to help dancers perform a particular sequence. You need not only to have figures of this kind in your head but in your feet as well!

How do people learn sequence dancing? Some just watch others going round but the majority attend group sequence dancing classes where the simpler dances are taught and practised. Most teachers run dances in addition to the teaching sessions, since practice and more practice is the secret of success. Given time the legs will move where they ought to go without too much thought. Perhaps one of the most satisfying aspects of modern sequence dancing (in addition to the music and the good company) is to be aware of the gradual improvement in performance over time - what seemed very difficult in the early stages becomes very simple as the months pass by.

Sequence dancing is essentially a practical activity and you may wonder why a book is needed. First of all it is nice to have some know-how of the background to dancing. You hear the experts discussing the mysteries of the hover cross and natural telemark - it is pleasant to be able to put in a word or two yourself. Secondly it is useful to have a manual to study away from the dancing sessions. It is hoped that the sequence dancers will use it as a reference book and dip into it from time to time as their studies progress.

Sequence Dancing and Ballroom Dancing

In sequence dancing all couples do the same steps at the same time. A popular sequence dance such as the Sindy Swing (written in 1984) has a set order of dancing figures arranged to fit a 16-bar sequence. Dances of this kind can be recorded in a dance script.

Ballroom dancing, in contrast, is a form of free-style or go-as-you-please dancing. The partners decide what steps they will do and in what order. In dancing a modern waltz they will turn right or left and do a chassé or change step as they see fit - there is no script.

Sequence dancers use the same music as ballroom dancers but there is an introductory section of 4 bars to ensure that the dancers start off together. The sequences are made up of steps and figures from ballroom dancing but there is much more interchange between the various dances. Thus the curved feather from the slow foxtrot is used in both the waltz and the quickstep. Although there are many similarities between sequence and ballroom dancing there are distinct differences - the two forms cannot even share the same floor for a quickstep!

Sequence Dance Scripts

Sequence dancing is a complex activity and even the simplest of dances is difficult to describe on paper. The man's and lady's steps are usually different and there are alignments, amounts of turn, timing, hand holds, etc. which need to be specified. The dance script is the approved method and such scripts are readily available for most of the dances now performed. Some examples will be given later in the book and also a list of suppliers.

Scripts are useful for learning and memorising dances and for sorting out difficulties with particular steps and some dancers subscribe to organisations which supply them with the scripts of new dances as soon as they appear. They are by no means essential, however, for the average sequence dancer and a thorough knowledge of dancing figures is far more useful.

Numbers of Scripts

The number of scripts available for any particular dance depends upon its age and popularity. The following table gives numbers and types of dances in one supplier's script list (more than 2,000 in all).

Sequence Dance	No. of Scripts	Sequence Dance	No. of Scripts
Tango (OT/Mod)	359	Samba	26
Waltz (OT)	253	Stroll	17
Waltz (Mod)	241	Glide	14
Saunter	200	Sway	14
Quickstep	157	Schottische	13
Slow Foxtrot	145	Set dances	13
Two Step	96	Mazurka	11
Blues	83	Party	10
Rumba	80	Paso	8
Cha Cha Cha	68	Parade	7
Swing	68	Bossa Nova	5
Gavotte	50	Polka	4
Jive	39	Miscellaneous	90

Old-time waltzes use different dancing figures and are played at 40-44 bars per minute; modern waltzes are played at 29-31 bars per minute. The differences in style between modern and old-time tangos are more subtle - these dances are classed together in this table.

No-one will ever know how many sequence dances have been arranged over the years. Estimates of 1,000 or more (!) new dances per year appeared in the December 1965 issue of 'Dance News' and several arrangers (including Ken Fuller) have more than 100 to their credit. Only a small proportion continue to be danced, however, and it is to be regretted that many excellent dances have disappeared into limbo.

4

The Development of Sequence Dancing

For many purposes a classification of sequence dances by age is very useful. A convenient system is to use 25-year units and make 3 classes:- Early, 1900-1949; Transitional, 1950-1974; Late, 1975 and after.

1. Early Sequence Dances - 1900-1949

Many old-time sequence dances were written from 1900 to 1920 and from 1950 onwards. In between there was a decline in sequence dancing although many Northern clubs kept up the old-time traditions. The period between the wars was the time of jazz and free expression - many strange dances came and went. The modern dances such as the modern waltz, slow foxtrot and quickstep were just beginning to emerge in something like their present form. Great efforts were made by the dancing authorities to bring some order out of the chaos. Dancing figures were standardised and a great emphasis was placed on technique. The "English" style of ballroom dancing, with its body contact, footwork, rise and fall, sway and contrary body movement, began to take shape - this is still the basic technique of the modern sequence dancing of today.

Early Sequence Dances 1900-1949			
Dance	Year	Dance	Year
Veleta	1900	Fylde Waltz	1902
Eva Three Step	1904	Military Two Step	1906
Gay Gordons	1907	Doris Waltz	1908
Boston Two Step	1908	Latchford Schottische	1909
Pride of Erin Waltz	1911	Dorothy Waltz	1912
L'Inspiration Gavotte	1914	Maxina	1917
Yearning Saunter	1919	Square Tango	1922
Royal Empress Tango	1922	Lingering Blues	1929
Hoop-a-La	1938	Rinking	1939
Breakaway Blues	1946	Waltz Cavalcade	1948
Harry Lime Foxtrot	1949	Oriental Mazurka	1949

Most of the dances listed are 16-bar sequences but the Latchford Schottische is 12 bars, the Maxina 24 bars and the Pride of Erin Waltz 32 bars.

Old-time waltzes, gavottes, two steps, schottisches, mazurkas, polkas and some glides are danced in the old-time style with the feet at an angle and steps are taken more on the toes. The sequences use dancing figures and terms derived from ballet with French names such as 'pas de valse' and 'rondé de jambe'.

Saunters, foxtrots, tangos, swings, blues and sways are danced in a more modern fashion with the feet in parallel position.

Some dances have a mixture of both styles. In the Boston Two Step the marching steps have the feet in parallel position not turned out; in the Moonlight Saunter some figures have the feet at an angle.

Some knowledge of old-time technique is essential to the modern sequence dancer since one third of new official sequence dances come from the old-time section. Again, it is not at all unusual for old dances like the Eva Three Step to be performed at a modern session, particularly at holiday times or on special occasions.

2. Transitional Sequence Dances - 1950-1974

There was a great revival in old-time dancing after the Second World War as older people took up again the dancing habits of their youth. Old time waltzes, two steps, mazurkas and gavottes appeared along with saunters, tangos, glides, strolls and sways and even square dances. As time went on, however, a more modern form of sequence dancing began to emerge. The old-time waltz was gradually replaced by the slower modern waltz and the two step gave way to the sequence foxtrot and quickstep. The process was well advanced by 1965 and by 1975 there were distinct differences between old-time and modern sequence dancing sessions.

Sequence dancing has always been very popular in the North and Chapter 15 written by Ken Fuller describes the history of the development of modern sequence in the Manchester region from 1950 to 1965 in some detail. As Secretary of the Manchester Area M.C's Club since 1956 and Editor of the 'Focus' club magazine, he has been well placed both to observe and make his own personal contribution to modern sequence. He has arranged scores of dance scripts and met many of the personalities of the Northern dancing world. He describes the issues of the day, the dances and their authors and manages to convey some of the excitement of these formative years.

Transitional Sequence Dances 1950-1974			
Dance	Year	Dance	Year
Eugene Tango	1950	Butterfly Gavotte	1950
Magenta Waltz	1951	Lilac Waltz	1951
Midnight Tango	1954	Waverley Two Step	1956
Mayfair Quickstep	1958	Idaho Foxtrot	1959
Jacqueline Cha Cha Cha	1961	Tango Serida	1961
Helena Quickstep	1962	Kingston Quickstep	1962
Melody Foxtrot	1963	Red Rose Tango	1963
Alana Foxtrot	1967	Universal Quickstep	1967
Tango Solair	1970	Balmoral Blues	1971
Rumba One	1971	Sally Ann Cha Cha	1973

Modern waltzes, slow foxtrots and quicksteps from early in this transitional period often show some of the characteristics of old-time dances such as saunters and blues. There is more repetition of dancing figures and partners may sometimes move to shadow hold or double hand hold or even perform solo turns. They also include dancing figures less fashionable today in these modern dances, such as the step and point, the twinkle, rotary turns and squares of various types. The later versions use standard figures and ballroom technique - ballroom hold, maintenance of body contact and no pronounced movement against the line of dance.

3. Late Sequence Dances - 1975 and after

In 1975 the Official Board of Ballroom Dancing (now the British Council of Ballroom Dancing) took tighter control of sequence dancing. All new (official) sequence dances since this date must be winners of an inventive dance competition licensed by the BCBD. Technique and composition of sequences for any particular dance such as an old-time or a modern tango are also controlled - if a new dance diverges too much from standard practice it will not win a prize in its section and hence not appear as a new official modern sequence dance.

Of the 45 new dances each year, 15 come from each of the following 3 sections:-

Old-Time - Old-Time Waltz, Old-Time Tango, Saunter, Blues, Swing, Gavotte, Two Step, Mazurka, Schottische, Glide, Sway, etc.

Modern - Modern Waltz, Modern Tango, Quickstep, Slow Foxtrot, Viennese Waltz.

Latin American - Rumba, Cha Cha Cha, Samba, Jive, Paso Doble, Bossa Nova, etc.

Late Sequence Dances 1975 and after			
Dance	Year	Dance	Year
Saunter Together	1975	Glenroy Foxtrot	1976
Rumba Aquarius	1981	Edwardian Gavotte	1981
Dixie Swing	1982	Karen Foxtrot	1982
Cameron Quickstep	1984	Sindy Swing	1984
Tina Tango	1986	Kontiki Quickstep	1986
Caribbean Foxtrot	1986	Saga Waltz	1988
Fantasy Jive	1989	Woodspring Quickstep	1989
Debbie Blues	1989	Chandella Quickstep	1990
Harlequin Foxtrot	1990	Westlynn Waltz	1990
Lakeside Rumba	1991	Torque Tango	1991
Commador Cha Cha Cha	1992	Bella Bossa Nova	1992
Jessica Jive	1992	Sandringham Saunter	1992
Jasmine Foxtrot	1993	Carliol Waltz	1993

Popularities of Various Types of Dance

The award-winning dances in order of popularity from 1981-1991 are set out in the following table:-

New Official Dances 1981-1991			
Dance	No. of Dances	Dance	No. of Dances
Tango (Mod & OT)	74	Swing	20
Waltz (Mod)	60	Blues	14
Rumba	55	Gavotte	13
Saunter	48	Samba	10
Cha Cha Cha	45	Waltz (OT)	10
Quickstep	37	Two Step	5
Jive	35	Others	2
Foxtrot	34	**TOTAL**	**462**

In advanced sequence dancing sessions the new dances are performed within a few days of their appearance. An analysis of one year's quota of 45 new dances might be something like the following:-

Tango (OT/Mod) 7; Mod. Waltz 6; Saunter 6; Rumba 6; Cha Cha Cha 5; Slow Foxtrot 4; Quickstep 3; Jive 3; with 5 more from Swing, Blues, Gavotte, OT Waltz, Two Step, Bossa Nova, etc.

Tangos and saunters (and to a lesser extent blues and gavottes) have been popular since the early days. (The modern staccato tango dates from round about 1935.) Swings came more into favour after 1968. Latin-American dances came to the fore in the 1970's - rumba from 1975, cha cha cha and jive from 1979.

It is not easy for a new type of dance to gain a foothold. Some dancers will sit out a samba, bossa nova, paso doble or even a jive since they feel that it is not worthwhile acquiring a technique for a dance that will only appear on rare occasions. There is male resistance in some areas to the more formal old-time dances such as the old-time waltz, gavotte and two step, particularly those involving bows and curtsies.

9

The Popularity of Sequence Dancing

In places where modern sequence dancing has caught on it must be the most popular form of social dancing yet devised. Within easy travelling distance of a medium-sized town (population, say 100,000) in one of these areas there may be 3 or 4 sequence dancing sessions each evening with occasional dances in the morning and afternoon. There are hundreds of regular dancers and an average attendance of 50 or more at a session is not unusual. Some dancers have been turning out several evenings per week for 20 years or more. Dancers can choose between an evening out with friends performing a few of the older sequence dances to a commitment of 7 nights per week mastering the new dances as they appear and working to improve their technique.

Some reasons for this enthusiasm are:-

(a) the wide range of dances available. There are more than 20 types of dance and thousands of sequence dances;

(b) many more different dancing figures can be used since leading by the man is less important than in ballroom dancing. Figures moving against the line of dance can be brought in since everyone is moving the same way;

(c) sequence dancing is easier to learn than dance forms with free expression since the steps are repeated many times in a set order. Dancing can be learned by observation and lessons are not essential;

(d) the new dances produced every year give life and interest to the movement. Sessions are crowded as soon as they appear.

Other important factors are:-

(a) the availability of cheap devices for playing recorded music. Any group can now come together for sequence dancing given a floor and a leader. Dancers can attend several dances per week without costs being prohibitive. These clubs have been a stabilising influence and have provided opportunities for newcomers to learn the art. Club dances have been invaluable in preserving the older dances and promoting the best of the new;

(b) the general improvement in the standard of living. Older people are in better health, have more time available and often have a car to get to outlying dances;

(c) the high standards of performance set and maintained by the various professional ballroom associations. These bodies provide qualifications for teachers and students, monitor new sequence dances and give a firm structure to the movement;

(d) the efforts of the hundreds of dedicated group leaders and teachers who turn up regularly (often without financial gain) to play the music and lead off the dances. Often they have to prepare the room and tidy up afterwards. They are truly the backbone of the sequence dancing of today.

Ballroom and Sequence Dancing Sessions Compared

Ballroom and sequence dancing are very closely connected but fundamentally very different. Sequence dancing is very popular among the people who like to dance and there are far more sequence dancing sessions than ballroom dances - trained ballroom dancers are something of an elite and there are not many places where there are enough to run dances every day of the week. Sequence dancing is somewhat of a down-to-earth folk activity - it lacks a lot of glamour of ballroom dancing. People in general do not go to watch sequence dancing apart from some of the competitions and inventive dance festivals. There is only one sequence dancing journal and very little literature available apart from the scripts. The popularity of sequence depends to a large extent on the community spirit engendered when people meet together frequently to pursue a common aim. When you first attend a sequence dancing session you feel that everyone is interested in you - they watch and evaluate how you perform and even where you sit! If you don't do a dance they like to know why. They all have the intention of moving round to the music in a friendly atmosphere - they watch one another to check that they are performing the sequences correctly. Watching is important in learning new dances and improving technique, and sequence dancers are rather good at it. In advanced sessions there is great competitive spirit - a new dance will come out on Monday and the enthusiasts like to have it mastered by Tuesday at the latest. Sequence dancers often go on sequence dancing holidays together and meet up outside the dancing sessions.

Ballroom dancing is a much more private affair - a close relationship between the dancing partners and a more distant relationship with the audience and other dancers. The man needs to lead the lady and if they are to perform more complicated figures they need to work out a sequence for themselves and practise it. A ballroom dancing session is really a number of couples all doing their own thing - partners are not interchangeable (as with sequence) once a certain level of expertise has been reached. (Note however that in simple ballroom dancing partners are very interchangeable and in the 1940's and 1950's it was all the go - many marriages started on the ballroom floor!) Ballroom dancers aim to do a limited number of dancing figures with good style according to the principles laid down by the various associations. They take private lessons, gain awards and enter competitions. Ballroom dancing is very attractive to watch - for many people it is a spectator sport verging on cabaret in some cases, e.g. 'Come Dancing' on the BBC. There are many teachers and schools of dancing - it has great respectability. There is a weekly paper and some journals and much literature and informed discussion. Unfortunately, it does not bring people out dancing on a regular basis like sequence, and some ballroom dancers have turned to sequence dancing with some reluctance. They like the dancing and the community spirit but feel that the general standard of the dancing leaves much to be desired. The ballroom-trained dancers exert a good influence in the sequence dancing sessions by performing the dances in proper style. Keen dancers will watch them and possibly pick up some of the finer points of dancing technique.

CHAPTER 2

LEARNING MODERN SEQUENCE DANCING

Choice of Learning Methods

Your first priority is to decide where you are going to do your dancing and acquire the necessary skills. This will obviously depend on what is available locally but you need also to think about your ultimate objective - is the dancing to be mainly a social activity or do you aim to master the dances as they appear and acquire a good style? Several approaches are available.

Social (club) dancers attend tea dances or dancing clubs where the older sequence dances are performed. They learn the dances by careful observation and following people as they dance round. They get by reasonably well without formal teaching, dance scripts or much else - these dancers often have a great talent for performing and remembering sequence dances. This method has its limitations - the number of dances that can be learnt is restricted and faults in style and performance may be picked up from other dancers.

By far the most common learning method is to join an elementary sequence dance teaching group. It is more or less assumed in this book that this is the route the majority will take. In these classes some of the easier and more popular dances are 'stepped through' and then practised by the class as a whole. The repertoire of dances is gradually extended with on-going instruction in technique and dancing style. Intermediate or improvers' classes include some of the simpler new dances whereas advanced classes teach the new dances as they appear. There is not always a sharp distinction between teaching sessions and dances - all sequence dance sessions have some type of learning element. Most leaders will 'step through' or call out the order of dancing figures for a new dance or an older one that has been partially forgotten unless the dance is a very formal occasion.

Some teachers give private instruction in sequence dancing in the period before the group dancing session starts. More rapid progress can be made and there are good opportunities to discuss difficulties and details of dancing technique. It is, however, more expensive and some slow learners may feel uncomfortable under the eagle eye of the instructor.

Another alternative is to take lessons in ballroom dancing. If the various dancing figures are learnt correctly it is not too difficult to adapt to modern sequence. Although there is much common ground between ballroom and sequence there are distinct differences. Ballroom dancers aim to execute a limited number of figures in a dance such as a waltz or quickstep with a classic style according to the principles laid down by the various dancing associations. They usually work towards examinations and many dancing manuals are written with this in mind. Ballroom dancers design their own sequences of dancing figures rather than following a set 16-bar sequence.

All sequence dancers must sooner or later give some attention to style of performance once they have passed the elementary stages. You cannot see yourself dancing unless you use a mirror or have a video taken and your best friends will be loathe to mention your faults. A teacher on the other hand will see your mistakes at a glance and have the authority to point them out to you. Teaching by a qualified ballroom dancing teacher is perhaps the only effective way to attain a really high standard.

A Time Scale for Learning

There are so many modern sequence dances that it is unrealistic to expect to master them all. A more reasonable aim would be to be able to attend any local session, holiday dance or sequence dancing festival without feeling too much out of place. To perform most of the dances with reasonable style and to follow the rest without being a nuisance to others - this is a standard attained by many but not without a good deal of effort and some anguish at times.

Some dancers will be hindered by lack of time, shortage of partners, physical disabilities, illness or lack of facilities in a particular area. It will also take longer if the basic skills of ballroom dancing have to be acquired. To be used to dancing with a partner and be able to transfer weight smoothly from one foot to the other is a great help to the aspiring sequence dancer. All things considered an average time of about 3 years seems about right with continuing improvements in repertoire of dances and style as the years pass by.

First Year (Elementary)

Progress is rather slow for the first few months while the first dances are being mastered. It may be a very frustrating period for a slow learner to see others getting on well - persistence is required here. When a repertoire of about 10 dances has been achieved it will be possible to get in more practice at other sessions and things will move along faster. A good selection of the older dances is very useful since they come up regularly on all sorts of occasions.

Second Year (Intermediate)

More of the same with the introduction of some of the newer dances. This is a rather unsettling time as it is difficult to find dancing sessions at the right level. You have gone beyond the elementary programmes of some of the clubs and not yet become proficient enough for the advanced sessions. Considerable determination is required at this stage as it is easy to become discouraged.

Third Year

If the first stages have gone well this is the time to try to master the new dances as they appear (some 45 per year). This process is simpler than might be thought if several evenings per week are available since the new dances are stepped through and played a great deal at the advanced sessions. Practice is certainly the secret of success - even the more accomplished dancers work harder as the new dances appear.

Repertoire of Dances

The number of dances in any couple's repertoire will vary from night to night with mood and circumstances. Average dancers might expect to learn some 50 dances per year making 150 at the end of the 3-year learning period.

The following figures refer to a recent modern sequence dancing festival.

Age of dance	Number of dances	%
Current year	55	47.0
1 year old	15	12.8
2 years old	9	7.7
3 - 10 years old	13	11.1
More than 10 years	25	21.4

The learning programme suggested here would cover nearly half the dances (current year) with possibly another quarter being accounted for by older dances learned in the first 2 years; the remainder could be attempted or sat out. Notice that the 13 dances played in the 3 - 10 years category were chosen from 327 new dances appearing in the period (only 1 in 25).

Choice of a Sequence Dancing Session

Where modern sequence dancing is well-established there may be as many as 3 or 4 sessions to choose from each evening within a reasonable catchment area. It is important for the aspiring sequence dancer to choose the right level - too low a standard leads to boredom and lack of progress, too advanced a programme will lead to waste of time by missing dances and discouragement. As dancers improve they need to raise their standard and there is the problem of breaking ties and leaving friends behind. Eventually a more settled programme will be established but the sequence dancing situation is fluid and places rise and fall in popularity.

Types of Sequence Dancing Session

Type	Notes
Tea dances	Elementary sequence dances with some ballroom dancing. Good for the beginner.
Dancing clubs and groups	Intermediate standard. Recorded music used. Dances led off by the organisers or other nominated couples. Entrance fee and a small annual subscription. Tea and biscuits often provided.
Licensed clubs	Elementary or Intermediate. Live music (usually organ). No leader. Often free if you sign in as a visitor. Bar, bingo and raffle.
Teaching and semi-teaching	Elementary, Intermediate or Advanced. Recorded music. Dances led off by the teachers. These sessions give practice in the dances taught.
Formal dances	Intermediate or Advanced. Live music. Have a leader/MC. Sometimes attended by dancing teachers with groups of their students.
Dancing holidays	Intermediate. Music recorded or live. Sightseeing in the day; dancing in the evening.
Sequence Dancing Festivals	Intermediate or Advanced. Teaching sessions in the morning and afternoon. Formal dancing sessions in the evening.

It is not always easy to find out where the dancing sessions are held - they are rarely advertised and libraries and information centres do not usually have a full list. The secret is to talk to as many sequence dancers as you can find and ask their advice!

First Steps in Learning to Dance

Once you have arranged which sequence dancing sessions to attend you can then give some attention to basic principles -this will increase your confidence and should in due course improve your dancing. To be a competent sequence dancer you need to feel and respond to the rhythm of the music by carrying out the steps correctly with good style. It is also most important to be able to remember what comes next in the sequences - much of the book is devoted to this problem. A brief treatment of style, technique and rhythm follows as an introduction to the dancing exercises - these prepare the ground for the performance of a simple sequence waltz. Finer points of technique are dealt with in Chapter 14.

Elementary Technique

Acquiring a good dancing style presents many problems to the beginner. Starting off the wrong way may set up faults which are difficult to eradicate. On the other hand too much thinking about technique may cause you to lose track of the sequence. It is perhaps best to remember a few basic principles of style and go ahead with mastering some sequence dances. When you are moving round reasonably well you can improve your technique by watching more accomplished dancers. Bear in mind, however, that if you have very high standards lessons from a good teacher are essential. You need an outsider to point out and correct your errors.

General Principles

(a) Be relaxed rather than stiff; don't sag at the knees.

(b) Hold your head naturally. Don't look down at your feet since this will spoil your balance and give a bad overall effect.

(c) Swing your legs from the hips rather than moving them from the knees.

(d) Keep your feet straight not turned out. Pass them close together when moving forwards or backwards.

Rhythm

Rhythm is the accent which occurs in a regular manner throughout a piece of music. Most people have some sense of rhythm - they can march in time to a military band and they tap their feet to a lively tune. Dancing is rhythm expressed in motion. A good dancer will bring out the mood and underlying rhythm of a dance by subtle movements of body, legs, feet and arms. If you lack a feeling for rhythm your progress will be slower although with patience and practice things should improve.

Beats and Bars

Music for dancing is written in sections of equal length called **bars**. The number of beats per bar is called the **time** of music. The **tempo** or speed is the number of bars played per minute (bpm); thus the modern sequence waltz has 3 beats per bar and is played at 31 bpm, the slow foxtrot has 4 beats per bar and is played at 30 bpm - see Chapter 12 for more details of playing speeds, times and time signatures.

The rhythm and character of a dance are determined by both the tempo and the emphasis given to particular beats. In waltzes the first beat in a bar is stressed; in a quickstep it is the first (strong) and the third (weaker).

Syncopation

Syncopation is the displacement of either the beat or the normal accent of the music. The Viennese Waltz (played at 60 bpm) is played with the second beat slightly in front of its strict tempo, giving the characteristic lilt to the music.

Syncopation in ballroom dancing is used in a wider sense to mean any departure from the normal rhythm. In the sequence waltz a hesitation such as the step and point gives two beats to one step whereas a chassé in a waltz involves two steps to one beat - these are forms of syncopation. A syncopated weave is carried out in fewer beats than the normal waltz weave. Syncopation is a common method of introducing life and variety into a sequence dance.

Practising Dancing Figures

Before actually taking any steps it is wise to try to get the rhythm of the dance into your head. If sequence waltz music is available try to pick out the three beats in each bar by tapping your hand or foot - give the first beat an extra hard tap to provide the emphasis. If music is not available, count "1,2,3" at a rate of about one beat per second placing more stress on the first beat.

The following exercises lead up to the performance of a simple sequence waltz. They require little space and can be carried out at home with or without a partner. Dancers often work through the steps on their own in checking out a dancing figure or reading a dance script and the exercises can be carried out by an individual without music. Bear in mind, however, that dancing with a partner is very different! As the ditty goes:-

> His tango was delightful.
> His waltzing was a dream.
> His quickstep couldn't be bettered.
> His foxtrot had to be seen.

> But he couldn't guide a partner.
> And that's the sorry tale.
> He was only a solo dancer.
> And a very frustrated male!

Turns in particular are by no means the same when carried out with a partner. The lady gives support and her steps influence the way in which the man balances and moves. The axis of rotation is somewhere between the two partners rather than on the man's foot. Technical matters relating to dancing turns are looked at in the following chapter.

Some Useful Abbreviations

LOD	line of dance	agst LOD	against line of dance
W	wall	DW	diagonal to wall
C	centre	DC	diagonal to centre
LF	left foot	RF	right foot
fwd	forward	bk	backward
S	slow	Q	quick

Line of Dance

The line of dance (LOD) is the normal anti-clockwise movement of couples round the ballroom. Anyone facing down the line of dance has the wall on his right and the centre on his left. (Notice that 'centre' used in this way does not mean the geometric centre of the room.) The reverse clockwise movement against the arrows is called 'against the line of dance' (agst LOD).

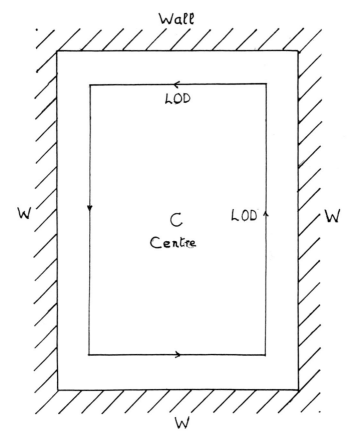

Notice that on turning the corner at the end of the room there is a new line of dance at right angles to the old line of dance - as before it has the wall on the right and the centre on the left.

Angle of Turn

In a complete turn the dancer faces the same way as before; after a half turn he will face in the opposite direction. In dancing, turns are divided into $\frac{1}{8}$ parts:- $\frac{1}{8}$ is 45°, $\frac{1}{4}$ is 90°, and so on.

A turn to face the right is a natural or clockwise turn.

A turn to face the left is a reverse or anticlockwise turn.

Dancers move round the ballroom in an anticlockwise direction making a turn of $\frac{1}{4}$ to the left at each corner.

Underturned and Overturned

Any dancing figure has a specified amount of turn - thus in the first three steps of the waltz turn the feet (and body) should turn through $\frac{3}{8}$. If less turn is made the turn is said to be underturned - if more, it is overturned.

1 2 3 Waltz Reverse Turn

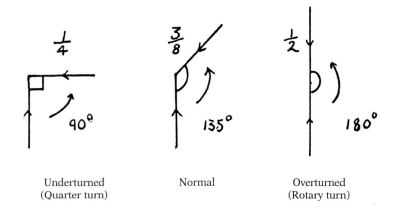

Underturned	Normal	Overturned
(Quarter turn)		(Rotary turn)

In dancing scripts the terms 'underturned' and 'overturned' do not always appear since the amount of turn is clear from the alignments of the feet (see Chapter 3) and space is often at a premium.

Exercise 1 - Walking in Waltz Time

Put on a recording of a sequence waltz (or count "1,2,3; 1,2,3" at about one beat per second if no music is available). Starting with your feet together move your weight forward and swing the left leg in front of you to take a walking step. Keep the body upright without being too stiff and do not look down at your feet. Follow with the right leg and so on. Place some emphasis on the first beat in each bar - perhaps you might make this step a little longer than the other two.

If you have a partner take her in ballroom hold and she will move backwards as you are moving forwards. Have the weight on the balls of your feet as you start to move forward - it is as though you were trying to push your partner over! Do not move the leg forward and then follow with the body -move your body forward as soon as the leg begins its motion. This forward poise is the basis of a good style. The body should be very slightly inclined forward from the feet upwards - do not bend forwards from the waist.

Now reverse the roles and try moving backwards - you will find this more difficult! Step back on to the toe. Swing your leg from the hips and do not lower the back heel until the other foot passes it.

The steps are set out in full and in abbreviated form below:-

Steps	Forward Walks		Beats
1	Left foot forward	(LF fwd)	1
2	Right foot forward	(RF fwd)	2
3	Left foot forward etc.	(LF fwd)	3

Steps for the backwards walks are opposite.

Forward walking steps are common in tangos, saunters, blues and swings. In waltzes the forward and backward changes are preferred (see later).

23

Exercise 2 - The Step and Point

In Exercise 1 there is one step to each beat. The step, point and hesitation figure introduces an element of syncopation into the forward motion.

Step forward with the left foot in time to the waltz music as before. Now move the right foot up to the left foot and touch the floor with the toe having the instep fully arched (the point). Do not put any weight on the foot at this stage. Hesitate for a beat and then step forward with the same foot (the right foot) on the first beat of the second bar. In this figure one foot is involved with three beats instead of each foot moving alternately.

Step and Point	Beats
1 LF fwd	1
2 Point RF fwd	2
3 Hesitate	3
4 RF fwd	1
5 Point LF fwd	2
6 Hesitate	3

(Man's steps; lady's steps are opposite)

The step and point is used in some old modern waltzes but is more common in saunters, swings and blues. Points are also used in tangos.

Another form of syncopation is to take two steps to one beat, counting as:-

1 and 2 3	1 2 and 3	1 2 3 and
Q Q S S	S Q Q S	S S Q Q

Examples are chassés and lock steps used in waltzes (see later).

Modern waltzes have syncopated zig-zags, locks, weaves, whisks and the quick open reverse turn. These are the normal figures with a slow step replaced by two quick steps.

24

Exercise 3 - Forward and Backward Closed Changes

Forward and backward walks in the waltz are rather unenterprising and are used only by beginners. The change steps are much more elegant and have a very long history. They are triangular in form and give a diagonal mode of progression. They are called change steps because they change the leading foot - thus the left foot leads in bar 1, the right foot leads in bar 2. As the man does a forward change, the lady does a backward change and vice versa.

	Forward changes	Backward changes	Beats
Bar 1	1 LF fwd 2 RF to side 3 LF closes to RF	1 RF bk 2 LF to side 3 RF closes to LF	1 2 3
Bar 2	4 RF fwd 5 LF to side 6 RF closes to LF	4 LF bk 5 RF to side 6 LF closes to RF	1 2 3

The feet are always closed together on the third step.

Left Foot Forward
Closed Change

(Man's steps)

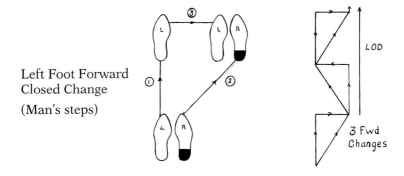

Notice that the left foot is placed slightly towards the line of the right foot. It is in CBMP (Contrary Body Movement Position) - see next chapter.

The Waltz Square

Amalgamations are combinations of two or more dancing figures. A waltz square is an amalgamation of the appropriate forward and a backward closed change.

A left-foot forward closed change followed by a right-foot backward closed change gives a clockwise waltz square.

Clockwise Waltz Square	Beats
1 LF fwd	1
2 RF to side	2
3 LF closes to RF	3
4 RF bk	1
5 LF to side	2
6 RF closes to LF	3

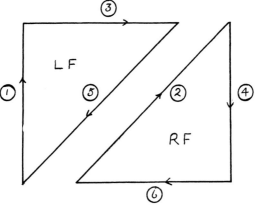

Man's steps; lady's steps are opposite

An anticlockwise square is a right-foot forward closed change followed by a left-foot backward closed change.

Practice both types of square using waltz timing. Square figures with a different timing of Slow, Quick, Quick, Slow Quick, Quick are often used in other dances (see later) - they are called chassé squares.

Exercise 4 - Quarter Turns and Reverse Waltz Squares

In the previous exercises the feet have always faced the same way - there has been no turning movement (no change in alignment). The following figures can be seen as closed changes with a quarter turn taking place on the second step. The turn of ¼ is less than the ⅜ turn on the first three steps of the standard turn in the waltz and these figures are said to be underturned.

The 123 Reverse Turn (Underturned) is a left foot forward closed change with a ¼ turn to the left. The 456 Reverse Turn (Underturned) is a right foot backward closed change with a ¼ turn to the left.

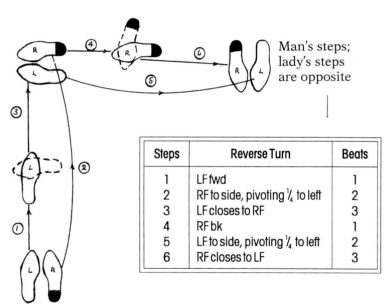

Man's steps; lady's steps are opposite

Steps	Reverse Turn	Beats
1	LF fwd	1
2	RF to side, pivoting ¼ to left	2
3	LF closes to RF	3
4	RF bk	1
5	LF to side, pivoting ¼ to left	2
6	RF closes to LF	3

Starting position ——

Notice that the triangular figure of the closed change has now become a straight line. Try these turns by yourself and with a partner; try also the opposite (natural) turns to the right.

27

Reverse Waltz Square

Two complete underturned reverse turns will give the reverse waltz square.

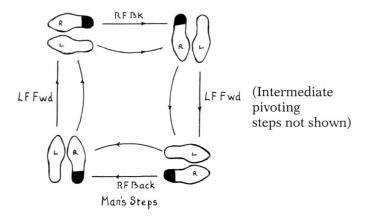

(Intermediate pivoting steps not shown)

Man's Steps

The turns and the square could well be
carried out in the opposite direction turning to the right instead
of the left giving a natural turn and natural square. The natural
turn is widely used but the natural square figure seems to go too
much against the normal anticlockwise motion round the
ballroom floor. It is however a good exercise to practice both
alone and with a partner.

Dancing figures are often symmetrical in form, e.g.:-

       (a) Natural turn forward
       (b) Natural turn backward
       (c) Reverse turn forward
       (d) Reverse turn backward

It is a great asset to be able to recognise and perform the four
forms comfortably and correctly.

For any given figure some forms are more popular than others.
This has been attributed to (a) the lady standing somewhat to
the right of the man making some turns easier and/or (b) the
natural right-handedness of the majority leading to a left-side
weakness.

Exercise 5 - Natural and Reverse Waltz Turns

In the standard waltz turns the feet turn through $\frac{3}{8}$ rather than $\frac{1}{4}$ as in the quarter turns. The man now needs to turn on step 3 as well as steps 1 and 2 since he is moving forward on the outside of the turn. On steps 4, 5 and 6 he is moving backward on the inside of the turn and he turns $\frac{3}{8}$ between steps 4 and 5 completing the body turn on 6. The situation for the lady is exactly opposite (see following Chapter 3 for more details).

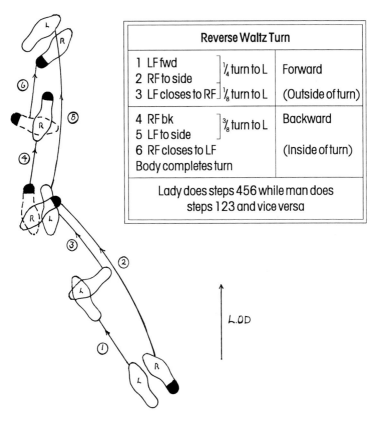

Reverse Waltz Turn		
1 LF fwd 2 RF to side ⎤ ¼ turn to L 3 LF closes to RF ⎦ ⅛ turn to L		Forward (Outside of turn)
4 RF bk 5 LF to side ⎤ ⅜ turn to L 6 RF closes to LF Body completes turn		Backward (Inside of turn)
Lady does steps 4 5 6 while man does steps 1 2 3 and vice versa		

L.O.D

Try this turn and the opposite natural turn by yourself and with a partner - they are by no means as difficult as they appear from the descriptions!

Exercise 6 - Rotary Turns

In modern sequence dancing the term "rotary" usually means a turn of $\frac{1}{2}$ instead of the standard turn of $\frac{3}{8}$ - it is overturned. Rotary waltz turns of this type with the feet in parallel position are found in some early modern waltzes. The following diagram of a natural rotary turn is taken from an old dancing manual.

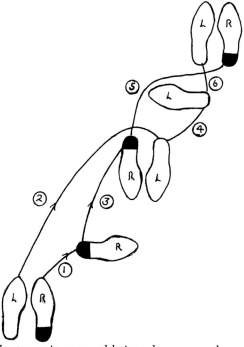

Rotary waltz turns in some old-time dances are danced with feet at an angle and have other differences - see Chapter 13.

The rotary chassé turn is a rotary turn adapted to sequences in 4/4 time by using a chassé timing of SQQ SQQ. It is found in saunters, swings and blues and some other old-time dances.

Try both the waltz and chassé rotary turns in each direction. You will find it necessary to swivel on both feet on the third and sixth steps. Although very simple in principle the amount of turn is rather too great for a really elegant figure.

Summary of Figures

Before attempting the Sweetheart Sequence Waltz it is a good idea to compare the dancing figures studied so far.

Figures in the Various Exercises	Notes
1 Forward and Backward Walks	No turn
2 Step and Point	Walks with hesitations, no turn
3 Forward/Backward Closed Changes	Triangular figures with the feet closed on the step 3, no turn
Waltz Square	Forward closed change followed by backward closed change repeated, no turn
4 123 Reverse Turn Underturned	Left foot forward closed change with turn. Straight-line figure, $\frac{1}{4}$ turn to left
456 Reverse Turn Underturned	Right foot backward closed change with turn. Straight-line figure, $\frac{1}{4}$ turn to left
Natural Turns Underturned	Opposite to the above, $\frac{1}{4}$ turn to right on each 3 steps
Reverse Waltz Square	123 and 456 reverse turns repeated, complete turn to left
5 123 Reverse Turn	Standard figure in the waltz, $\frac{3}{8}$ turn to left
123 Natural Turn	Standard figure in the waltz, $\frac{3}{8}$ turn to right
6 Natural Rotary Turn	123 natural turn overturned, $\frac{1}{2}$ turn to right 456 natural turn overturned, $\frac{1}{2}$ turn to right

The Sweetheart Waltz (Bars 1-14)

Time ¾, tempo 30 bpm. Start in normal ballroom hold, man facing down LOD. Man's steps; lady's steps are opposite.

	Counts	Steps	Figures
Bar 1	1	LF fwd down LOD	Step point
	2,3	Point RF fwd	
Bar 2	1	RF fwd down LOD	Step point
	2,3	Point LF fwd	
Bar 3	1	LF fwd	
	2	RF to side	
	3	LF closes to RF	Clockwise
Bar 4	1	RF bk	square
	2	LF to side	
	3	RF closes to LF	
Bars 5-8		Repeat bars 1-4	

(In all the above figures the man is facing down LOD.)

Bar 9	1	LF fwd tng L	
	2	RF to side along LOD	
	3	LF closes to RF fcg C	
Bar 10	1	RF bk still tng L	Reverse
	2	LF to side	waltz
	3	RF closes to LF fcg agst LOD	square
Bars 11,12		Repeat bars 9,10 to finish facing down LOD	
Bar 13	1	LF fwd down LOD	
	2	RF fwd	Forward
	3	LF fwd (check)	and
Bar 14	1	RF bk	backward
	2	LF bk	action
	3	RF bk	

The Sweetheart Waltz (Bars 15 and 16)

Bar 15	1	LF to side (check)	Check to
	2	Replace wt to RF	whisk
	3	LF crosses behind RF	
Bar 16	1	RF fwd (small step)	R foot for-
	2	LF to side	ward closed
	3	RF closes to LF	change

Notes on the Sweetheart Waltz

Bars 9-12   The reverse waltz square is an amalgamation found in older dances such as the Emmerdale Waltz and Cathrine Waltz. Not all scripts divide the turn into four quarters. Some do a reverse rotary turn ($\frac{1}{2}$) followed by a backward closed change (no turn); this is then repeated. This gives a narrow rectangle rather than a square. Other scripts use turns of $\frac{3}{8}$, $\frac{1}{8}$, $\frac{3}{8}$ and $\frac{1}{8}$ to give the complete turn. Many sequence dancers seem to turn to the left as seems most convenient to them and use the last three steps to make sure they are facing the right way. Reverse squares and waltz squares are rarely used in more modern sequence waltzes.

Bars 13/15   The **check** is a step in which the body movement is arrested and then reversed. In some scripts the checks are replaced by **hovers** in which the transfer of weight from one foot to another and back again is taken with a floating action rising on the toes.

Bar 15   The **whisk** step here is the crossing of one foot behind the other.

For most of the Sweetheart Waltz the man is facing down the line of dance with the lady opposite. This avoids the problem of diagonal alignments (see Chapter 3) and is one of the reasons for choosing this dance as a learning exercise.

Exercise 7 - Varying the Rhythm

You will find that if you walk in time to any sequence dance music you can do it at two speeds. The walk with quick (Q) steps is twice as fast as the walk with slow (S) steps. Neither walk is particularly attractive on its own and most sequence dances use a mixture of quick and slow steps to vary the rhythm and provide variety. The 'Slow, Slow, Quick, Quick, Slow' of Victor Silvester can be made the basis of four useful exercises. Notice that they have 4 beats to the bar (S = 2 beats, Q = 1 beat).

Bar	Timing	Step	1 Three Step	2 Chassé	3 Lock Step	4 Progressive Side Step
4	S Q Q	10 9 8	RF fwd LF fwd RF fwd	 9 LF closes to RF	 9 LF crosses behind RF	 9 LF to side
3	S S	7 6	LF fwd RF fwd			
2	S Q Q	5 4 3	LF fwd RF fwd LF fwd	 4 RF closes to LF	 4 RF crosses behind LF	 4 RF to side
1	S S	2 1	RF fwd LF fwd			

The three step is one of the basic figures in the slow foxtrot. The chassé and lock step are used in the quickstep and cha cha cha as well as in the waltz and other dances. The progressive side step occurs in some tangos. Notice that these are all change steps - they change the leading foot as well as the rhythm. (See 'Syncopated Change Figures' in Chapter 6.)

Try all these exercises both forward and backward. Try putting two chassés together and two lock steps together.

Exercise 8 - Chassé Figures

Many of the waltz figures described in the exercises can be carried out with a chassé timing: S Q Q instead of S S S.

The forward and backward changes become cross chassés and the waltz squares become chassé squares. The natural, reverse and rotary waltz turns become natural, reverse and rotary chassé turns.

123 Reverse Chassé Turn (Man's steps; lady's steps are opposite)	Timing
1 LF fwd tng L	S
2 RF to side still tng	Q
3 LF closes to RF	Q
Normal turn ³/₈; Quarter turn (underturned) ¹/₄; Rotary turn (overturned) ¹/₂.	

The reverse waltz square becomes a reverse chassé square. The Suzanne Quickstep starts with a reverse chassé square.

The Square Tango (1922), Melody Foxtrot (1963), Rumba Royale (1964), Sindy Swing (1984) and Bella Bossa Nova (1992) have clockwise chassé squares. The Moonlight Saunter (1919) and the Eugene Tango (1950) have anticlockwise chassé squares; the Nightfire Tango (1992) has an anticlockwise chassé square in shadow position (called a 'box' in the scripts). The Festival Glide (1957) has both types of squares in a figure of eight.

Try out these figures and look out for them in the various sequence dances which come up in your dancing sessions.

The script of the Square Tango which follows has two chassé squares and two three steps. (Sometimes the two 'three steps' are replaced by two 'progressive side steps'. The two right foot forward steps in bars 10 and 11 are then replaced by two right foot side steps.)

Square Tango (1922) - Old-Time

Time 2/4, tempo 32 bpm. Waltz hold facing down LOD. Lady dances counterpart.

CLOCKWISE SQUARE. SIDE STEP WITH DRAG CLOSE. FIGURES REPEATED.

Bar 1	LF fwd		S	
	RF to side		Q	
	LF closes to RF		Q	Clockwise
Bar 2	RF bk		S	Chassé
	LF to side		Q	Square
	RF closes to LF		Q	
Bar 3	LF to side (long step)		S	L Side Step
	RF closes to LF ww		S	Drag Close
Bar 4	RF to side (long step)		S	R Side Step
	LF closes to RF ww		S	Drag Close
Bar 5-8	Bars 1-4 repeated			

TWO WALKS, THREE STEP, WALK, THREE STEP, TURN AND CHECK, ROCK TURN.

Bar 9	LF fwd		S	Walks
	RF fwd		S	
Bar 10	LF fwd		Q	
	RF fwd (small step)		Q	Three step
	LF fwd		S	
Bar 11	RF fwd		S	Walk
	LF fwd		Q	
	RF fwd (small step)		Q	Three step
Bar 12	LF fwd		S	
	RF fwd tng ¼ R to face W		S	
Bar 13	LF to side		S	Turn and
	RF bk and check		S	check
Bar 14	LF fwd tng R		S	
	RF to side still tng		S	
Bar 15	LF to side still tng	L leg	S	Rock
	RF to side still tng	bhd	S	Turn
Bar 16	LF to side still tng	body	S	
	RF bk now fcg LOD		S	

36

Dancing the Tango

The main **modern** dances are the modern waltz, the slow foxtrot, the quickstep and the modern tango. They are called 'modern' since they are danced in the modern ballroom (or English) style - ballroom hold is used and body contact maintained at all times. The modern waltz, foxtrot and quickstep have similar footwork, rise and fall and sway - these aspects of technique are dealt with in Chapter 14.

The modern tango is the 'odd one out' and there are some things you could look out for when watching the experts perform this dance:-

(a) the hold is more compact, with the lady further to the right; her left hand is more towards the underside of the man's arm and may even rest on his back just below the arm pit;

(b) the feet are picked up slightly from the floor and 'stepped' into position, not swung from the hips as in the other three dances;

(c) the knees are flexed more than in the other dances and steps are taken at the last moment giving a crisp, staccato action;

(d) the tango is an intense, dramatic, masculine dance leaving no room for levity. There are exaggerated, quick motions of the head and other members of the body;

(e) the partners stand obliquely to the line of dance with the man's right hip and shoulder forward - this makes the walks curve slightly to the left (see Chapter 3 for details);

(f) there is no rise or fall or body sway and the shoulders should be kept level. Since there is no rise the ball of the foot is used in the scripts rather than the toe.

Old-time tangos, like the Square Tango, use many of the same figures as modern tangos but are not restricted to ballroom hold and other holds and solo turns are permitted. They are played at more or less the same tempo as the modern version but performed with a less staccato action. They are danced with feet in parallel position and have some affinities with saunters and blues.

Review of Chapter 2

Much basic material has been covered in this chapter and it merits careful study. Carrying out the exercises should have given some appreciation of rhythm as well as providing a simple introduction to dance figures and scripts.

The abbreviations used save much space and make the steps easier to follow. A knowledge of these is fundamental to understanding the charts appearing later in the book. More abbreviations are given in Chapter 3 and certain matters of technical interest are discussed; some finer points of technique are dealt with in Chapter 14.

A major problem in sequence dancing is remembering the steps. This is most conveniently done by having a thorough knowledge of the dancing figures and being able to perform them with ease. The two sequence dances so far described are best remembered by the order of their dancing figures:-

Sweetheart Waltz - Two Steps and Points. Clockwise Square. Figures repeated. Reverse Waltz Square. Forward and Backward Walks. Check to Whisk. Forward Closed Change.

Square Tango - Clockwise Chassé Square. Side Step with Drag Closes. Figures repeated. Two Walks. Three Step. Walk. Three Step. Turn and Check. Rock Turn.

Remembering sequence dances is considered at some length in Chapter 4. If you can remember the sequences of the majority of the dances that come up and dance them with good style and correct timing, you are well on the way to becoming a modern sequence dancer!

CHAPTER 3

ABBREVIATIONS AND TECHNICAL MATTERS

This chapter is a reference section for the remainder of the book; it might well be skipped over in a preliminary reading.

Abbreviations

acr	across	mvg	moving
ag, agst . .	against	opp	opposite
bhd	behind	OP	outside partner
bk(g)	back (backing)	PO	partner outside
br(g)	bring(ing)	posn . . .	position
cls(g)	close (closing)	prep(g) . .	prepare(ing)
comm(g) . .	commence (ing)	PP	promenade
cv(g)	curve (curving)		position
C	centre	prog	progressive
CBM	contrary bnody movement	prom . . .	promenade
		ptg	pointing
CBMP . . .	contrary body movement position	ptnr	partner
		Q	quick
		R	right
CPP	counter promenade position	RF	right foot
		RH	right hand
		rev	reverse
diag	diagonal(ly)	rsd, rsg . .	raised, raising
dn	down	S	slow
DC	diagonal to centre	sdw	shadow
		shldr . . .	shoulder
DW	diagonal to wall	s-by-s . . .	side-by-side
		sltly	slightly
fcg	facing	sq	square
fwd	forward	ss	small step
ldg	leading	swiv(g) . .	swivel(ling)
L	left	trans . . .	transfer
LF	left foot	twds . . .	towards
LH	left hand	tn, tng . .	turn(ing)
LOD	line of dance	ww	without weight

39

PP: Promenade Position - The partners are in a V-shaped position with the man's right side near the lady's left side. In Fallaway Position man and lady are moving backwards; the angle apart is slightly greater.

CPP: Counter Promenade Position - This is promenade position with the man's and lady's positions interchanged.

OP: Outside Partner - A forward step taken outside the partner instead of in line - usually taken to the right.

CBM: Contrary Body Movement - Turning the opposite hip and shoulder to the direction of the step being taken, e.g. as the left foot moves forward so do the right hip and right shoulder. The momentum for turns in dances like the waltz and quickstep comes largely from the "swing" of the opposite hip and shoulder; this effect is particularly marked in pivot turns. CBM is a body movement and is not mentioned in dance scripts.

CBMP: Contrary Body Movement Position - The foot is placed on or across the line of the stationary foot (either in front or behind) without turning the body. It gives a similar appearance to CBM without the body movement. It is a foot placing and appears in scripts and dancing figures (see following pages). CBMP is used on every outside step and step with partner outside to maintain body contact; it is found in some other figures such as the change in direction in the foxtrot.

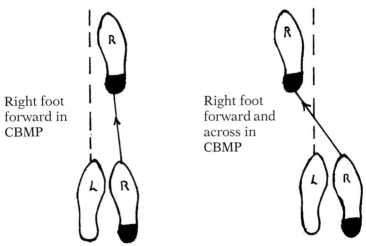

Right foot forward in CBMP

Right foot forward and across in CBMP

40

Foot Movements from a Parallel Position

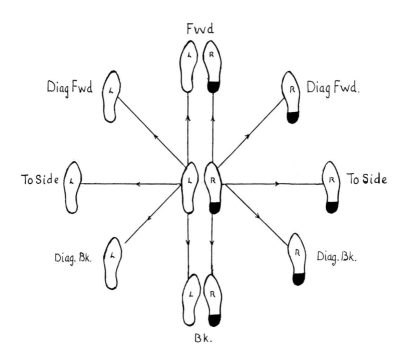

Intermediate Positions

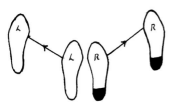

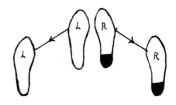

To side and
slightly forward

To side and
slightly backward

41

Alignments

In modern dancing the alignment gives the orientation of the foot to the line of dance when the step is completed. When feet and body are in line there are two alternatives for each direction:

(a) **Facing (fcg)** is the forward direction through the toe; used when the figure is moving forward, e.g. fcg LOD when the next step is forward.

(b) **Backing (bkg)** is the direction through the heel which is used when the figure is moving backward, e.g. bkg agst LOD.

Pointing (ptg) is used when feet and body are at an angle.

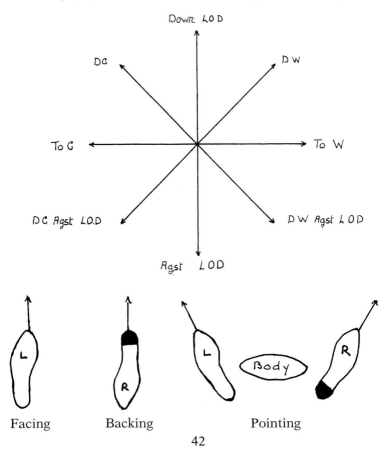

Amount of Turn

Positions in the ballroom and turning angles are very simply related.

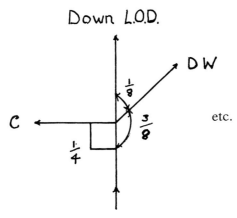

The amount of turn in dance scripts is usually indicated by the difference between the initial and final alignments of the feet. This is rather more complicated than the simple case above since the angle depends upon (a) whether the turn is to right or left, (b) whether the feet are facing or backing e.g. fcg C is the same direction as bkg W. Two examples will be given to illustrate this:-

(a) 123 Reverse Turn (e.g. waltz)

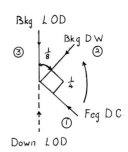

123 Reverse Turn (Man's steps)	
Step	Alignment
1 LF fwd	Fcg DC
2 RF to side	Bkg DW
3 LF closes to RF	Bkg LOD

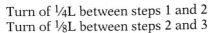

Turn of ¼L between steps 1 and 2 } Total turn
Turn of ⅛L between steps 2 and 3 } of ⅜L

(b) 1234 Quarter Turn (Quickstep)

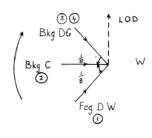

Quarter Turn (Man's steps)	
Step	Alignment
1 RF fwd	Fcg DW
2 LF to side	Bkg C
3 RF closes to LF	Bkg DC
4 LF to side sltly bk	Bkg DC

Turn of ⅛R between steps 1 and 2 } Total
Turn of ⅛R between steps 2 and 3 } turn
No turn between steps 3 and 4 } of ¼R

In charts of dancing figures the amount of turn is usually indicated both by the angle turned through and the changes in alignment of the feet.

Starting Alignments for Figures

Each dancing figure starts and finishes with a particular alignment and it is most important to observe these to dance easily and correctly. Notice that the initial alignments for the figures in the last section are:-

(a) 123 Reverse Turn	Fcg DC (for a left turn)
(b) 1234 Quarter Turn	Fcg DW (for a right turn)

In each case this initial turn of ⅛ from facing the line of dance helps the turn on its way.

The finishing alignment will determine what figures can follow - thus the 1234 quarter turn finishes bkg DC and can be followed by a progressive chassé, quarter turn to the left or reverse pivot. In sequence dances the order of figures is already determined but it is useful to know how they fit together - this is particularly useful in reading the script of a new dance.

Starting Sequence Dances

Starting with the correct alignment is a great help in performing the dance smoothly and easily. The starting alignment depends upon the hold, the nature of the dance and the starting figures.

1. **Partners Facing** e.g. ballroom or open facing hold.

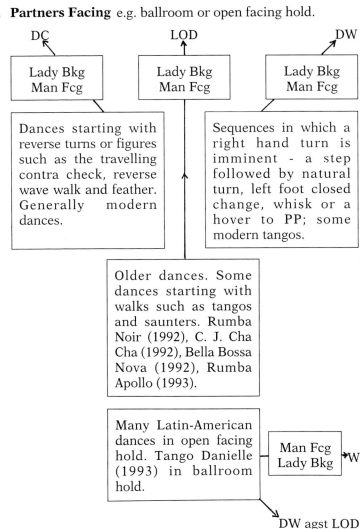

DC | LOD | DW

Lady Bkg
Man Fcg

Lady Bkg
Man Fcg

Lady Bkg
Man Fcg

Dances starting with reverse turns or figures such as the travelling contra check, reverse wave walk and feather. Generally modern dances.

Sequences in which a right hand turn is imminent - a step followed by natural turn, left foot closed change, whisk or a hover to PP; some modern tangos.

Older dances. Some dances starting with walks such as tangos and saunters. Rumba Noir (1992), C. J. Cha Cha (1992), Bella Bossa Nova (1992), Rumba Apollo (1993).

Many Latin-American dances in open facing hold. Tango Danielle (1993) in ballroom hold.

Man Fcg
Lady Bkg

W

DW agst LOD
(Invicta Rumba, 1993)

45

In nearly all these dances the starting steps are:-

Man LF fwd ; Lady RF bk

(Exceptions are the Aurora Foxtrot (1989), man LF bk; Invitation Swing (1983), man RF fwd.)

2. Partners Side-by-Side

The usual position for partners starting in shadow position or old-time side-by-side position is facing down LOD. Even if the dancers are at an angle to one another in promenade position or old-time open hold, their general direction is down LOD.

A few dances start facing DW.

Shadow hold - Taurus Tango (1991), Shimmering Gavotte (1991), Social Samba (1992).

Open promenade position - Popcorn Samba (1991).

In all these dances the man starts LF fwd. Sometimes the lady's step is RF fwd but in shadow hold she may take the same step as the man, that is LF fwd. This is called dancing on the same foot (on same leg). Many dances in side-by-side position have some steps of this kind. The Samba Marina (1990) and the Grenadier Two Step (1993) are danced on the same foot throughout.

Dancing Turns

Figures involving turns are among the most complex likely to be encountered in modern sequence dancing. Steps for man and lady are often quite different at different stages of the turn. These problems increase as the angle of turn gets larger - for turns less than one quarter the lady's steps are often just the plain opposite of the man's steps. Problems with turns arise from a number of factors - need to maintain body contact for leading purposes, line and appearance to onlookers, comfort in performance, etc. There is also a physical factor relating to the distance travelled during the turn referred to as being on the inside or outside of a turn.

Inside and Outside of a Turn

In many dancing turns there is a forward or backward movement along the ballroom as well as a turning motion (a progressive and a rotary action). In such turns the partner moving **forward** on the **outside** of the turn moves further than the person moving **backward** on the **inside** of the turn.

This is easily seen by looking at a diagram of a rotary half turn. For both man and lady there are three steps:- 1. Fwd turning; 2. Side turning; 3. Closing step. The distance is covered in the two strides on steps 1 and 2; the third step moves the body into line.

The distance apart of the bodies will be the sum of distances 'a', 'b' and 'c'. On average this will be about 1ft. for the half turn and correspondingly less for turns through a smaller angle. The forward step will thus be 1ft. longer than the corresponding backward step and this will be independent of the step length:-

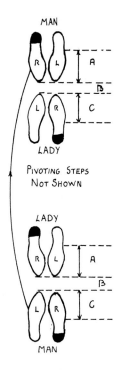

e.g. Forward step 3ft.
    Backward step 2ft.
    Forward step 2ft.
    Backward step 1ft.

If the lady takes short steps when she moves forward on the backward half of a turn, the man's step must be shorter still.

Put in very simple terms, it is harder to turn when moving forward than when moving backward. Thus in a simple turn such as 1. Step, 2. Step to side, 3. Closing step, the turn has to be made over all three steps when moving forward whereas when moving backward the turn is made over the first two steps with the body completing the turn on the third step.

47

There are many examples throughout the text; e.g. natural and reverse waltz turns - Exercise 5, Chapter 2, p. 29; chassé quarter turns - Chapter 8, pp. 92, 93.

The general rules to remember are:-

(a) Moving forward on the outside of a turn - turn more slowly and travel further. Stretch the side step.

(b) Moving backward on the inside of a turn - turn more sharply and travel less.

For larger amounts of turn to reduce these problems there are at least two possibilities:-

(a) Swivel with man's and lady's feet closer together as in the telemark turns; these are more or less turns on the spot.

(b) Pivot on one foot, step to the side and pivot in the same direction on this foot also - this will achieve some progression.

More about CBMP

CBMP is a foot position in which the moving foot is placed on or across the line of the stationary foot without turning the body. It is an inward leg movement tending to lock the legs together above the knee. It gives the appearance of CBM without moving the body - the opposite hip and shoulder seem to be turned to the direction of the step being taken.

Shoulder leading is the opposite of CBM - the same side of the body moves with the stepping foot. It is an opening-out movement which can be taken either forward or backward. It alters slightly the direction of the step and is mentioned in dancing figures and scripts. Shoulder leading steps and steps in CBMP often follow one another - one reverses the effect of the other. Shoulder leading is usually used prior to a step outside partner.

Two examples are given below:-

(1)

Feather Step		Timing
Man's Steps	Lady's Steps	
1 RF fwd	1 LF bk	S
2 LF fwd L shldr lead preparing to step OP	2 RF bk R shldr lead	Q
3 RF fwd in CBMP OP	3 LF bk in CBMP	Q
4 LF fwd partner square	4 RF bk partner square	S

A slight opening-out to the left on step 2 is followed by a most elegant step 3 in CBMP outside partner. Bodies come back into line on step 4.

(2)

Forward Walk (Modern Tango)	Timing
Man's Steps	
1 LF fwd in CBMP DW curving sltly L	S
2 RF dn LOD R shoulder leading	S

The locking of the upper parts of the legs on step 1 is followed by an opening-out movement to the right on step 2. The starting position is Man fcg DW; Lady bk DW. (The steps are sometimes abbreviated to 1 LF fwd DW; 2 RF fwd dn LOD).

The body turning effects in shoulder leading and CBMP are relatively small. Much more pronounced movements occur in other figures. Examples of cross-body figures are the outside checks in the chair, New York and shoulder to shoulder; opening-out movements are the natural fallaway and the hand to hand in rumba and cha cha cha.

Review of Chapter 3

Modern sequence dancing - or, indeed, any form of dancing -is very complex when looked at in detail. Describing the various dancing figures is like trying to instruct someone how to tie a shoelace in writing! Fortunately, (as with the shoelace) it is easier to do than to set down on paper.

As the dancing skills improve there is more opportunity to consider the finer points of sequence dancing. It is hoped that dancers will study the reference material in this chapter from time to time as their expertise increases.

To sum up:-

(a) Abbreviations are very necessary to save space and time in writing out scripts and dancing figures. They are soon mastered by reading through the list and working away at a few of the dancing figures.

(b) A thorough knowledge of foot alignments is essential for reading dance scripts. Having the correct starting alignments for starting the dance and the various figures will make your dancing easier and more attractive to watch.

(c) Dancing turns pose some practical and theoretical problems. It is hoped that angle of turn and the concept of the inside and outside of turn will be made clear by looking at the examples. Remember to take smaller steps when moving backward on the inside of a turn - this will help you both to get round.

(d) CBMP presents difficulties for some dancing students. A careful study of the Feather Step should do much to help here. No attempt has been made to treat another form of CBMP - Can't Budge My Partner!

CHAPTER 4

REMEMBERING SEQUENCE DANCES

Learning can be seen as putting information into the memory store, remembering is taking it out again. In modern sequence dancing these processes are probably more important than in any other form of social dancing - it is, at one and the same time, the attraction and the major problem for the sequence dancer. Ballroom dancers can decide to some extent what steps and figures they will perform and in what order - they may change their minds at the last moment if approaching a corner or are short of space. A sequence dancing pair, in contrast, needs to perform the steps in the order and manner determined by the dancing script - any departure from the norm will be a cause of frustration to the partners and a source of confusion to others. No amount of style or grace or technical expertise will compensate for a failure in this area. This is what keeps the sequence dancers on their toes!

Once the appropriate skills have been mastered, sequence dancing should be a natural pleasant process not requiring too much use of the mind. Overmuch use of the mind may work against the memory process.

"The centipede was happy quite until the toad in fun
said "Pray which leg comes after which?"
This brought her mind to such a pitch
she lay distracted in the ditch considering how to run!"

A common mistake among learners is to try too hard, leading to a tense and jerky performance - an accomplished dancer will miss a few steps when in trouble and gradually ease back into the sequence. Notice how many very able sequence dancers go to pieces when asked to lead off - they can do the dance perfectly well but the occasion overwhelms them; they concentrate too hard and disaster follows. What the sequence dancer needs is some sort of remembering process which does not require too much mental effort. Practice is the real secret of success but there are various ways of using the mind to help the feet to go where they should.

Different Types of Memory

People vary tremendously in their retentive and remembering skills. Some people remember tunes well and can play by ear; some professional musicians have prodigious memories and can play for hours without a musical score. Others have a good pictorial memory and can accurately reproduce images they have seen by drawing or painting. Football enthusiasts can tell you who played in the teams of years ago and the scores in the various matches. Ballet dancers and champion skaters need the ability to remember long complicated sequences of body movements. If you have this God-given ability you have no need to study this chapter.

Learning processes in sequence dancing are mainly visual:- the steps are observed, the dance performed and the information stored away in a neat and tidy manner in the brain. Some people have normal (or above average) intelligence with a good memory for many things and yet a poor memory for foot movements. These people have a different cognitive style - they will still need to watch the steps very carefully but the information needs to be stored and interpreted in a different manner for them. The method suggested in this book is to translate the movements into dancing figures and to build up a framework of theory which will make the foot movements easier to remember.

A Memory Model

A useful model is to consider the brain as containing a framework or gestalt for sequence dancing purposes. Information will flow in from the eye, by listening to the music and hearing the voice of the dancing teacher, and from the movements of the legs and body whilst dancing. This will be stored away and classified over time (particularly during sleep) and interrelations will build up between the incoming data and information stored elsewhere in the brain. When the right stimulus is applied the information can be recalled - this is **remembering**. Thus if all is well with the system, when you hear "Balmoral Blues" the proper responses will be elicited and the feet will do what they should.

The exercises in Chapter 2 can be used to show how a learning framework can be developed using dancing figures. The foot movements are associated with the figures which are then interrelated to give something that can be added to and improved by study away from the dancing sessions.

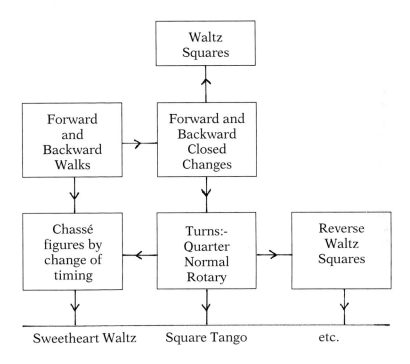

For many people it is useful to have some picture of the figures in the mind or some other means of recognition.

Thus:-

Closed Changes	-	Triangular figures
Waltz Turns	-	Closed changes with a turn
Waltz Turns	-	Step, Step, Close

Some tips for learning sequence dances are:-

(a) Take every opportunity to watch dancers carefully - you can learn also from people who make mistakes!

(b) Try and translate the movements into the appropriate dancing figures and study them from a book when you get home.

(c) Relate the dancing figures to one another to help memory and recall - look for similarities between the various dances.

(d) Take a record of the dancing figures for a new dance or record the steps in some way that appeals to you.

(e) If you are really keen, obtain the appropriate dancing scripts and use them to sort out difficulties with particular steps.

Above all, get as much practice as you can and work hard at the learning process.

Recalling Sequence Dances

Even when you can do all the new dances with ease and have a good selection of the older popular dances your problems are not at an end! The memory framework is there all right but can you remember the right button to press to elicit the desired performance? If asked to lead off can you recall the sequences which you have practised to perfection and performed many times? Dance leaders and teachers have this problem in an acute form. Study of scripts and practice beforehand either at home before the dance (or even in the corridor outside during the dance) are all used to ensure a good performance on the night. One partner may whisper the figures to the other during the dance - two heads are better than one!

Another widely-used method is by **association** - the use of a key word, phrase or idea to unlock the stored memories. This is sometimes called a "memory jogger"; some examples are given below:-

1. Unusual Steps or Figures

- the aerial turn in the Eugene Tango (1950);

- the double chassés and quick run on the toes in the Eivona Quickstep (1974);

- the swivels in the Kontiki Quickstep (1986);

- the hinge in the Charminster Waltz (1989) and Waltz Clinique (1991);

- the hand on shoulder forward chassés in the Mahogany Cha Cha Cha (1992) (The Elephant Dance);

- the two changes of direction in the Stardust Foxtrot (1993).

2. Comparing Dances in General Terms

- the Tiara Tango is the Square Tango (1922) backwards;

- the Red Rose Saunter (1991) is the Together Saunter (1975) with lock steps;

- the Atlanta Rumba (1992) has a Turkish towel at the beginning and ends something like the Lakeside Rumba (1991).

Vague ideas of this kind often stick in the mind and many dancers use these methods of recall.

3. Comparing Sequences in Different Dances

(a) Dancing teachers will often point out that the middle sections of the Woodside Waltz (1964) and Emmerdale Waltz (1979) are very similar. The sequences are:-

Whisk Wing, Open Telemark, Hover, Contra Check.

Of the 48 steps in the 2 dances, 14 are virtually the same.

(b) The Lancaster Tango (1987) and the April Foxtrot (1992) have:-

Open Telemark, Double Fallaway, Same Foot Lunge, Turning Four Step (or Five Step).

(c) Similar starting sequences:-

  (i) forward basic, alemana, hand to hand, followed by walks or lock steps (many cha cha chas).

  Sally Ann (1973), YC (1976), Corrida (1990), Susie Q (1992) Cha Cha Chas.

  (ii) 123 reverse turn and progressive chassé often followed by a natural turn.

  Cameron Quickstep (1984), Quatro Quickstep (1991), Linden Swing (1992), Waltz Daniella (1976), Wensley Waltz (1990), Denverdale Waltz (1992), Waltz Cerise (1993).

Since there are only a limited number of dancing figures and new dances keep appearing, there must be some repetition of popular sequences. Even experienced sequence dancers find comparisons between dances of this kind most helpful - it is a most pleasant experience in learning a new dance to go down some well-trodden track with the steps well classified in the mind.

Recording Sequence Dances

The sequence dance script is the standard method for transferring information. When the new dances appear you may see the dancing teachers looking at cards or sheets with lists of steps. Really keen sequence dancers subscribe to one or other of the commercial organisations that supply new scripts on a regular basis.

You will often see dancers taking their own record of a dance. When duplicating information was more difficult teachers used to keep records of the dances in small notebooks. Steps are often put down in very abbreviated form and different people have their own particular methods.

Pictorial Methods of Recording

One system of recording sequences of movements in ballet called Labanotation (Rudolf von Laban (1928)) uses vertical lines running up the page with symbols for the various steps and figures. Right hand side body movements are recorded on the right side of the centre line, left hand side movements on the left. A related system for sequence dances has been developed by Thomas Scott of Dunfermline called Q-dancing (1972).

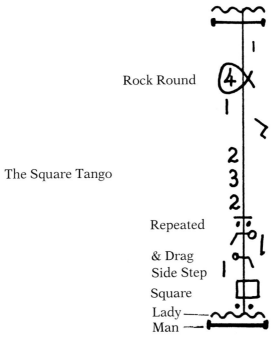

Forward steps are in black, backward steps in red. Squiggles are used for turns and a circle for a closing step. Dancing figures are crystallised into simple characters which suggest the pattern of the movement and save many words. An important part of the system is that large charts of the dances should be available for all to see to help their performance. Q-dancing methods were used in Scotland for several years for teaching sequence dancing. Dancers might like to exercise their ingenuity in devising their own systems to save space and words.

A Cautionary Note

Dancing figures are valuable aids to memory and performance but they have their peculiarities. Do not just go by the name of the figure - check up the steps to be sure. It is often thought (and said!) that ballroom figures are set out in detail in a big book available only to highly qualified teachers. Unfortunately the dancing authorities have not yet reached this measure of agreement and the standard manuals vary - the reverse corté in the waltz may have 3 or 6 steps; the quickstep quarter turn 4 or 8 steps; the three step in the slow foxtrot may start with left or right foot. When you hear "Reverse Corté", check up which version they are using!

These minor problems are made worse by arrangers needing to split up figures for the sequences, faulty descriptions, typing errors, poor naming of figures and sometimes mistakes by the dance leader. Look out for the following:-

Zig-Zag - often only a 'zig' which is a type of quarter turn like the start of a turning four step.

Walking steps - may be turning steps as in the Chevy Swing (1993).

456 Reverse turn - usually underturned and often not much more than a closed change.

Open natural turn - is it a natural waltz or quickstep turn taken from promenade (open) position or a turn with feet passing one another as in the slow foxtrot?

Tipple chassé - is this the backward quarter chassé turn to right (Chapter 9) or any type of chassé with a sway?

Snippets of figures - e.g. 9-11 running right turn as in the Katy Quickstep (1993); correct but not particularly helpful.

Alternative names - three step used for curved three step or even curving feather; three forward lock steps may be called three forward chassés or three forward cha cha chas.

More about dancing figures appears in the following chapter.

CHAPTER 5

STANDARD DANCING FIGURES

Modern sequences are largely made up from standard figures from ballroom dances and these will now be considered.

Dancing figures are groups of steps ranging in size from the 1 step of the Reverse Pivot in the quickstep to the 30 steps of the Turkish Towel in the cha cha cha. **Standard figures** for a particular dance have been selected by ballroom dancing experts as being the best for general usefulness, style of performance and teaching purposes. They are the basis for the system of ballroom dancing awards and qualifications for both modern and Latin-American dances. Not all dancing associations have exactly the same lists of standard figures and there are minor differences of detail but in the main there is substantial agreement on content.

Each dance has its own dancing figures and these are described in **charts** which give the positions of feet, footwork, alignment, amount of turn, rise and fall, CBM, sway and timing. Figures to precede and follow each movement are listed with suitable explanatory notes. In the dancing manuals the standard figures are often set out in sections of increasing difficulty corresponding to the associate, member and fellow awards. The standard figures and their accompanying technique have been developed and refined over more than seventy years and ballroom dancing now rests on a firm theoretical basis.

Old-time dancing is treated in a rather different way. There are no standard figures as such but sets of steps such as the pas de gavotte and pas de basque; there are movements like twinkles, sways, rocks, solo and rotary turns commonly found in old-time dances such as saunters and blues. The standard work is 'A Guide to the Theory and Technique of Sequence (Old-Time) Dancing' compiled by the Sequence Advisory Commmittee of the Official Board of Ballroom Dancing (now the BCBD). This booklet gives hints on technique and explains the various terms used in old-time sequence dancing.

Numbers of Dancing Figures

The British Council of Ballroom Dancing Rule Book for 1993 gives the following numbers of standard figures for the Modern (Standard) and Latin-American Dances:-

Modern Waltz 23, Modern Tango 20, Quickstep 25, Slow Foxtrot 20, (Viennese Waltz 5), Rumba 30, Cha Cha Cha 28, Jive 23, Samba 19, (Paso Doble 26).

Excluding the Viennese Waltz and Paso Doble, there are 188 figures. Adding 12 figures for the old-time dances gives a round number of 200 dancing figures to form the basis of the modern sequence dancing of today. In addition there are some figures called **variations** used by advanced ballroom dancers and a number of movements peculiar to the sequence dances themselves. A competent sequence dancer has to perform these figures correctly as they appear in the dance scripts in the appropriate modern, Latin-American and old-time style. This is a big undertaking but easier than it might appear. (It is no small task either to describe it in print in readable form in a limited space!)

Methods of Classifying Dancing Figures

The **ballroom method** used in most dancing manuals considers each dance in its own right - thus the slow foxtrot has a certain walk and style and dancing figures of its own. There is little emphasis on similarities between figures in different dances as this is not important to the ballroom dancer who aims to perform a limited number of figures in a small range of dances with great style and elegance. This treatment is adequate for the advanced sequence dancer who has a good grasp of the figures and can use the charts to correct small errors in his technique. It is much less satisfactory for the beginner to modern sequence - there is too much detail and the range of dances and figures is restricted. The explanatory notes refer to ballroom dancing technique rather than modern sequence and there is no treatment of saunters, blues and swings. Similar figures in different dances have different names and sometimes varying numbers of steps - this does not matter much to a ballroom dancer but is a source of confusion to the aspiring sequence dancer.

The **new approach** to dancing figures was first set out in the author's previous book 'Modern Sequence Dancing: A New Approach' (1992). Dancing figures are classified not by dance but by similarities in foot movements. If a dancing figure is to be found in several dances it seems appropriate to set out the essential features of the figure and then consider how it is used in the various sequences. This approach cuts down the mass of material to be remembered and brings more order and reason into the sequence dancing process. Remembering sequences is a major problem to the sequence dancer - a good technique and style are of little value if the feet are going awry. If the dancers can remember the foot positions and the basic shape of a figure they can pick up the timing from the music (and the better dancers around them) and hope to improve their technique with practice.

Similarities between Dances

Ballroom dancers are well aware that there is considerable overlap between the 200 or more standard figures used in modern sequence dancing. Thus one dancing manual lists 10 figures common to the waltz, foxtrot and quickstep (with different timings) and another 4 common to the tango also. Ballroom teachers would argue (quite rightly) that there are distinct differences between, for instance, the telemark turn in the waltz and the foxtrot. The basic issue in proposing a classification of figures by foot movements is thus whether or not there is sufficient underlying similarity between the dances to justify this approach. Some arguments in favour of the new system are set out below:-

(a) There is no doubt that the various dances in modern sequence seem very different in atmosphere - the quickstep is lively, the rumba sensual and the foxtrot slow and elegant - this is one of the greatest attractions of modern sequence dancing. These differences can however be attributed largely to differences in tempo and how the different beats are accentuated. Apart from waltzes which are played in triple time, music for most dances is written in 4/4 time (or occasionally 2/4 time which does not sound much different to the average dancer). There is always some emphasis on the first beat in the bar; the other beats are stressed to different extents in the various dances. The underlying foot movements and the shapes of the figures are very similar in the different dances although performed with different timings.

As a change, sequence dances are sometimes played to different rhythms.

Sequence Dance	Alternative Rhythm
Rumba Rosalie	Jive
Sindy Swing and	Cha Cha Cha, Samba
Mayfair Quickstep	and Two Step
Tango Serida	Viennese Waltz

The dancers seem to move round comfortably enough in the alternative styles suggesting that the dances differ more in tempo and accentuation of beats rather than order of steps. It will sometimes happen that the wrong dance music is put on for a particular sequence dance. It is surprising to see how well the dancers have moved round in many instances before the mistake is noticed!

(b) Many old-time sequence dances finish with bars of waltzing. The dancers move round readily enough whether the time signature is 3/4 for waltz, 4/4 for the gavotte or 6/8 for the military two step. They use the same dancing figures but change the timing.

(c) Dancing figures often transfer readily from one dance to another. Chassés are used in waltzes, the contra check and zig zag in the tango. The check on either side of partner is found (under various names) in waltzes, foxtrots, rumbas and cha cha chas as well as in the Mayfair Quickstep.

Considering the advantages to be gained by looking at the figures in this new way the new approach seems to have some merit. The following chapters will examine dancing figures in this way in order of increasing difficulty.

CHAPTER 6

WALKS AND CHANGE FIGURES

Forward and Backward Walks

Forward walking steps are an important feature of tangos, saunters, blues and swings. Each 4-bar section of the Kingfisher Saunter (1990) starts with 2 forward steps. Walks are slow steps often used in the middle of a dance to give time for readjustment after a complicated turning figure. In foxtrots the walking steps are usually included in the foxtrot figures.

Although the forward walk is the simplest of all dancing figures this does not mean that it is easy to perform well. It has been said that the basis of good dancing is a sound technique for the forward and backward walks.

Backward walks are more difficult to perform than the modified walking action of the forward steps. It is not easy to maintain poise and balance whilst taking a long enough backward step.

Different styles of walk are needed for the different dances:-

Waltz - Sweeping and gliding movements with the whole body. There is a gradual rise from the first to the third step.

Slow Foxtrot - Steps slightly longer than in the waltz. The slower tempo means that good balance is required.

Quickstep - Shorter and quicker steps than in the foxtrot. It is important not to overstride on the long steps and snatch at the quick steps. Side steps should be short.

Tango - Bold, firm steps of natural length with no up and down movement. The knees are slightly flexed and there is no gliding motion - the feet are picked up slightly and set down heel first. Movements should be staccato and taken late on the beat. In the modern tango many steps are taken with strong contrary body movement.

63

Rumba - Short, heavy, walking steps taken more from the legs and feet than in gliding dances such as the waltz and slow foxtrot; there should be a smooth, supple hip motion.

Cha Cha Cha - Slow and staccato steps with neat and precise footwork. There should be less hip movement than in the rumba - no bouncing up and down.

Samba - A peculiar flat-footed sort of walk in which the dancer moves forward and then pulls back with a sway of the upper body making progress rather slow. The samba has a bouncing or bobbing movement initiated by a springy knee action.

Jive - Another dance with a 'bouncy' action. All the steps are taken on the ball of the foot with the heel off or just touching the floor.

One Step and Two Step - Marching military walks taken with a straighter leg than in the normal ballroom walk. Many of the other steps are performed with feet at an angle.

Some dances have special walks of their own such as the Kiki walks in the rumba and the chicken walks in the jive.

Change Figures

Change figures change the leading foot - in general they are figures with an odd number of steps. Natural turns and many other figures start on the right foot and if these occur at the start of a sequence at least **one** preliminary step is needed. The Universal Quickstep (1967) and Kay's Quickstep (1991) have a left foot walk followed by natural turn. The Alana Foxtrot (1967) and Sahara Foxtrot (1991) have a left foot walk followed by a feather.

In waltzes, **three step** figures such as the forward closed change are more commonly used instead of the single step. The Waltz Clinique (1991) and Sophie's Waltz (1993) have a left foot forward closed change followed by a natural turn.

Waltz changes are among some of the oldest of the dancing figures. The pas de valse in the old-time waltz is used for moving from a natural to a reverse turn and vice versa. It is a three step with the feet closed on the third step danced with the feet at an angle; it can be taken forward or backward with either foot (see Chapter 13).

Forward and Backward Closed Changes

These are triangular three step figures with feet closed on the third step; they give the modern waltz its diagonal motion (see Chapter 2). Many social dancers replace these changes with forward walks and lose the opportunity of performing a very graceful waltz figure. Many 123 turns are completed by a backward closed change - this is often called a 'closed finish'.

The Outside Change

The outside change is a standard figure in the waltz; it involves a $\frac{1}{4}$ turn to the left without the feet being closed at any stage. It occurs in the Waltz Babette (1968) and Charminster Waltz (1989). In the Blue Lace Waltz (1991) it is finished in promenade position and reverses the action of the curved feather; these two figures are then repeated. The Abbeydale Foxtrot (1983) has an outside change.

Outside Change		Outside Change to PP	Timing
Man's Steps		Man's Steps	
1. LF bk in CBMP		1. Partner on right side	S
2. RF bk	$\frac{1}{4}$	2. Partner turned square	S
3. LF to side, sltly fwd	turn	3. In promenade position	S
(pointing step)	to L		

Passing Changes

These are backward three-steps with a $\frac{1}{8}$ turn. They are 'open' figures like the outside change - the feet pass one another instead of closing, e.g. Westgate Waltz (1987). The Stardust Waltz (1989) has a syncopated passing change.

Change of Direction

The change of direction is a standard figure in slow foxtrots and quicksteps, e.g. Sahara Foxtrot (1991), Chandella Quickstep (1990). The Stardust Foxtrot (1993) has two changes of direction each preceded by a weave. Notice that the second step is an opening-out movement with a shoulder lead; the left foot closes to the right foot **without weight** (ww).

Change of Direction		Timing
Man's Steps	**Lady's Steps**	
1. LF fwd ⌐ ¼	1. RF bk ⌐ ¼	S
2. RF diag fwd, R shldr ‖ turn	2. LF diag bk, L shldr ‖ turn	S
ldg, LF closes to RF, ‖ to	ldg, RF closes to LF, ‖ to	
sltly fwd ww ⌐ L	sltly bk ww ⌐ L	
3. LF fwd in CBMP	3. RF bk in CBMP	S

Summary

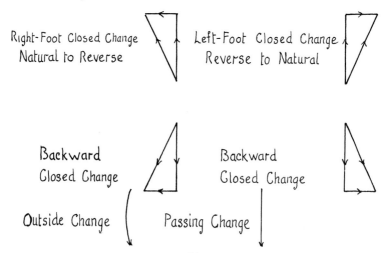

Right-Foot Closed Change
Natural to Reverse

Left-Foot Closed Change
Reverse to Natural

Backward
Closed Change

Backward
Closed Change

Outside Change

Passing Change

Syncopated Change Figures

In simple change figures all the steps are slow. Bringing in quick steps or a hesitation to give a syncopated figure changes the rhythm as well as the leading foot.

	Beats	1	2	3	4
1.	**Simple change**	LF	RF	LF	RF
		Three step change (in 3 beats)			
2.	**Quick change**	LF	RF LF	RF	LF
		S	Q Q		
		Three step change (in 2 beats)			
3.	**Hesitation change**	LF	RF	RF	LF
		Hesitation			

Notice that '2' and '3' are out of step with '1' after the first two beats.

Changes in rhythm of this kind are used to different extents in the various dances. The modern tango with its staccato action has S = 1 beat, Q = ½ beat and also ¼ beat steps in such figures as the syncopated lock step (Q and Q; ¼,¼,½) The rumba, on the other hand, is danced to 2 3 <u>4 1</u> (QQS) where Q = 1 beat, S = 2 beats with rarely any change in rhythm.

The three step, chassé, lock step and progressive side step in Exercise 7, Chapter 2, p. 34 are examples of syncopated change steps. Leaving out a change step such as a chassé or twinkle will put the dancer out of step with everyone else - standing on the foot that is needed to move on - a common problem for the learner! In this situation a hesitation is usually better than rapid quick steps - it does not look so 'jumpy' and attracts less attention.

Some of these syncopated three steps will now be looked at in more detail.

The Three Step

The three step starting with the right foot is possibly the most important figure in the slow foxtrot. Just as the chassé is used in the quickstep and waltz to change the rhythm so does the Quick, Quick, Slow of the three step give the foxtrot its special characteristics.

Three Step		Timing	
Man's Steps	Lady's Steps	Foxtrot	Others
1. RF fwd	1. LF bk	Q	S
2. LF fwd	2. RF bk	Q	S
3. Rf fwd	3. LF bk	S	S

The three step may be started with the left foot or taken in a backward direction, e.g. bar 14 of the Melody Foxtrot (1963). The Eva Three Step (1904) consists largely of three steps followed by a point taken in forward, backward and sideways directions.

The Feather Step

The feather step consists of a slow walking step followed by a three-step starting with the left foot. It is a most elegant step in which the man steps outside the lady on the second quick step and then moves back in line (see Chapter 3, p.49).

Feather Step		Timing
Man's Steps	Lady's Steps	
1. RF fwd	1. LF bk	S
2. LF fwd, L shldr lead preparing to step OP	2. RF bk R shldr lead	Q
3. RF fwd in CBMP OP	3. LF bk in CBMP	Q
4. LF fwd partner square	4. RF bk partner square	S

Many turns and figures have a 'feather ending' or 'feather finish' consisting of the last three steps of the feather. The feather can be taken from promenade position (Tempro Foxtrot (1992)). 'Feather' generally implies some movement outside the partner (see also Hover Feather, Chapter 7, pp. 78, 79).

The Progressive Side Step

This is a forward three step with the second step is taken sideways; it should curve to the left. It is a standard figure in the tango and involves a quickening of the tango walk.

Progressive Side Step		Timing
Man's Steps	**Lady's Steps**	
1. LF fwd in CBMP	1. RF bk in CBMP	Q
2. RF fwd to side, sltly bk	2. LF to side, sltly fwd	Q
3. LF fwd in CBMP	3. RF bk in CBMP	S

The **progressive side step reverse turn** is the above figure with a strong turn to the left followed by a step forward with the right foot, often taken against the line of dance (Glendale Tango (1991)).

Curved (Curving) Three Steps and Feathers

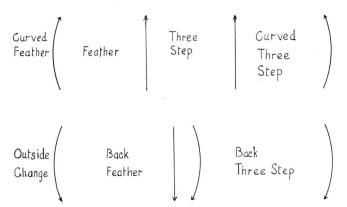

Curved (Curving) Three Step

This is a three step with up to ¼ turn to the **left**. In the Sahara Foxtrot (1991) there is a curving three step in which the man has to turn the lady and move in line; this figure requires good technique. The Westlynn Waltz (1990) has a curved three step in which the man walks round the lady on the left; the Saga Waltz (1988) has 3 backward curving walks.

Curved and Back Feathers

A **curved feather** consists of the first three steps of the feather curving up to $\frac{1}{4}$ turn to the **right**. It is usually followed by a backward movement.

Examples are:-

Nevada Foxtrot (1990) followed by a curved back feather;
Sahara Foxtrot (1991) followed by an open impetus turn;
Blue Lace Waltz (1991) followed by an outside change to PP.

Curved Feather		Timing	
Man's Steps	**Lady's Steps**	**F**	**W**
1. RF fwd $\frac{1}{8}$ turn	1. LF bk $\frac{1}{8}$ turn to R	S	S
2. LF diag fwd, to R	2. RF bk	Q	S
L shldr ldg, $\frac{1}{8}$	R shldr ldg		
prep to step OP turn	$\frac{1}{8}$ turn		
3. RF fwd in CBMP OP to R	3. LF bk in CBMP ss to R	S	S

F=Foxtrot/W=Waltz

A **back feather** occurs in the April Foxtrot (1992).

Back Feather		Timing
Man's Steps	**Lady's Steps**	
1. LF bk in CBMP	1. RF fwd in CBMP OP	S
2. RF bk, R shldr ldg	2. LF fwd, L shldr ldg	Q
3. LF bk in CBMP	3. RF fwd in CBMP OP	Q

A **curved back feather** has a $\frac{1}{8}$ turn to the right over the three steps (Nevada Foxtrot (1990)).

The Twinkle

Quick and slow twinkles are standard figures in social rhythm dancing. The twinkle is used in saunters, swings, tangos and other types of sequence dance. It is a type of change step like the chassé and the three step - leaving out a twinkle will leave the dancer on the wrong leading foot. Twinkles may be started with either foot or taken forwards or backwards.

Right Forward Twinkle		Timing	
Man's Steps	Lady's Steps		
1. RF fwd	1. LF bk	Q	S
2. LF closes to RF	2. RF closes to LF	Q	S
3. RF bk	3. LF fwd	S	S

Adding a fourth step closing the feet together gives the closed twinkle. The Columbine Saunter (1991) ends with a left forward closed twinkle, timed Q, Q, Q, Q. The Cheney Blues (1992) has a backward twinkle with close whilst the lady does circling walks - this is repeated with the roles reversed.

Remember that if you have a good twinkle you might become a star!

Hesitations

A **hesitation** is a pause in a figure in which the weight is retained on one foot for more than one count. Hesitations sometimes include a **drag step** in which one foot is closed to the other without weight, e.g. Square Tango (1922) (Chapter 2, p. 3), Roxy Quickstep (1991) and the end of Border Waltz (1992). Another form of hesitation involves the dancer standing on one foot whilst the other leg does a kick, swing, point or one or more taps. (The Step and Point in Exercise 2, Chapter 2, is an example.)

The **Hesitation Change** is a rapid method of moving from 1 to 3 of the natural turn to 1 to 3 of the reverse turn. After the natural turn steps, the man steps back with his left foot and slowly pulls his right foot towards it (heel pull). After a slight hesitation he goes into the reverse turn as in the Woodside Waltz (1964) and Eivona Quickstep (1974).

The Drag Hesitation

In the waltz this figure is often followed by a back lock (Rose Lane Waltz (1963), Waltz Louise (1989)). It is used in the April Foxtrot (1992).

Drag Hesitation		Timing	
Man's Steps	**Lady's Steps**	**W**	**F**

1. LF fwd ⎤ ¼ turn to L
2. RF to side ⎦
3. LF closes ⎤ ⅛ turn to L
    to RF ww ⎦
	1. RF bk ⎤ ¼ turn to L
	2. LF to side ⎦
	3. RF closes ⎤ ⅛ turn to L
	    to LF ww ⎦
		S
		S
		S
			S
			Q
			Q

W=Waltz/F=Foxtrot

The Cross Hesitation

The cross hesitation is often used as a finish to the open telemark and open impetus turns.

Cross Hesitation		Timing
Man's Steps	**Lady's Steps**	

1. RF fwd in CBMP OP
    (pointing step)
	1. LF fwd across ⎤
	    IN CBMP and PP ¼ turn
	    (pointing step) to L
		S

2. LF closes to RF ww 3. Position held	2. RF to side ⎦ 3. LF closes to RF ⅛ turn to L	S S

A cross hesitation followed by a back lock is found in the Blue Lace Waltz (1991).

CHAPTER 7

CHECKS, ROCKS AND HOVERS

Reversing Movements

A **check** usually involves a change in direction from a forward to a backward movement with the weight being replaced to the back foot. The Harlequin Foxtrot (1990) has a checked feather, the Alana Foxtrot (1967) has a checked weave in bars 3 and 4. The first step in the basic movement of rumba and cha cha cha is sometimes described as a checked forward walk.

Rocks are a type of check in which the forward and backward movement is usually repeated. The rock should be made with the body without the feet being too firmly planted. Rock turns are common in tangos.

In **hovers** the checking action is carried out with a floating movement, the weight being transferred from one foot to the other rising on the toes. Hovers are graceful figures used in slower dances such as the waltz and foxtrot.

The **cucaracha** (beetle-crusher) used in the rumba has a very different action from the hover. It is a pressure step consisting of three steps, the feet being closed on the third step. It is often taken sideways with part weight (1. LF to side with part wt; 2. Replace wt to RF; 3. Close LF to RF).

The **lunge**, as the name implies, is a long step made longer by bending the knee of the other leg. The **same foot lunge** is found in many sequence dances: Kingfisher Saunter (1990), April Foxtrot (1992), Hadrian's Waltz (1992). The man's foot moves sideways whilst the lady's same foot moves backwards.

Some reversing movements do not involve a transfer of weight and two steps are taken with the same foot. A preliminary step is followed by a **point** (Sindy Swing (1984)) or a **flick** (Sharron Swing (1990)) or a **swing** in low aerial position (Singapore Swing (1992)).

Contra Checks

Contra checks and whisks are often used in waltzes and foxtrots to move in and out of promenade position to give variety. The Bellerby Waltz (1991) starts with a travelling contra check; the Tempro Foxtrot (1992) starts with a whisk and feather ending. The progressive and promenade links are figures used in the tango for this purpose.

The **contra check** is a standard figure in the waltz (Emmerdale Waltz (1979), Apple Blossom Waltz (1992)). It is also used in the tango with a SQQ timing (Tango Solair (1970), Tango Negro (1992)).

Contra Check		Waltz Timing
Man's Steps	**Lady's Steps**	
1. LF fwd in CBMP (pointing step)	1. RF bk in CBMP	S
2. Replace wt to RF	2. Replace wt to LF	S
3. LF to side in PP	3. RF to side in PP	S

In making the first step some weight should be retained on the right foot. The body should turn towards the left on the first step and to the right on the second step. This figure is taken with the partner in line ('contra' means 'against').

The **travelling contra check** is a contra check with the second step replaced by the right foot taking a small step to the side and slightly forward; the body is turned slightly to the right (Claudia's Waltz (1991), Denverdale Waltz (1992)).

Outside Checks

Checks outside the partner followed by a chassé or side step are found in many sequence dances - see Chapter 11, The Rumba and the Cha Cha Cha.

Side Step — Cathrine Waltz (1956), Westlynn Waltz (1990), Caribbean Foxtrot (1986).

Chassé — Mayfair Quickstep (1958), Sindy Swing (1984).

The **chair** is a sort of inside check in promenade position.

The Chair	Timing	
Man's steps; lady's steps are opposite	**F**	**W**
1. LF to side in PP along LOD 2. RF fwd and across in PP/CBMP, knees flexed 3. Replace wt to LF	Q S Q	S S S

F= Foxtrot/W=Waltz

The Glenroy Foxtrot (1976), Carousel Saunter (1991) and Blue Dawn Waltz (1991) have chairs with different timings. In the Cameron Quickstep (1984) the chair is called a check in PP. The **fencing line** is a type of chair in which the partners' joined hands are forward and the other arms held out backwards in fencing position (Rumba One (1971), Renaissance Rumba (1992), Commador Cha Cha Cha (1992)).

Progressive and Promenade Links

The **progressive link** is used in the tango instead of the travelling contra check to move into promenade position. It consists of the first two steps of the progressive side step with the lady being turned into promenade position.

Progressive Link		Timing
Man's Steps	**Lady's Steps**	
1. LF fwd in CBMP	1. RF bk in CBMP ⎤ ¼ turn ⎦ to R	Q
2. RF to side, sltly bk in PP, body turns to R	2. LF to side and sltly bk in PP	Q

This figure has become more popular with the introduction of the more staccato action of the modern tango. It is used in the Glendale and Torque Tangos (1991).

The **promenade link** is used to change from a promenade figure into a forward figure such as a four step or progressive side step.

Promenade Link		Timing
Man's Steps	**Lady's Steps**	
1. LF to side in PP	1. RF to side in PP	S
2. RF fwd and across in CBMP and PP	2. LF fwd and across in CBMP and PP ⎤ ¼ turn	Q
3. LF to side ww (small step)	3. RF to side ww (small step) ⎦ to L	Q

The promenade link is found in the Tango Debonaire (1990) and Tango Negro (1992).

Rocks

Open rocks have the legs apart, closed rocks have the legs in CBMP. They may start with either foot and be taken backward or forward or to the side. The rock is often taken with the man moving backwards against the line of dance (see following figure).

Left Foot (Open) Rock	Tango Timing
Man's steps; lady's steps are opposite	
1. LF bk, L shldr leading	Q
2. Transfer wt fwd to RF, R shldr leading	Q
3. LF bk, L shldr leading (small step)	S

Rocks are found in the Renaissance Rumba (1992), Telecon Tango (1992), Sacha Swing (1991).

The Natural Rock Turn

Natural Rock Turn		Timing
Man's Steps	**Lady's Steps**	

1. RF fwd, R shldr ldg ⌉ ¼
 2. LF to side, sltly bk ⎮ turn
 3. Transfer wt fwd to RF, ⎮ to
    R shldr leading ⌋ R
	1. LF bk, L shldr ldg ⌉ ¼
	 2. RF fwd, sltly to R ⎮ turn
	 3. LF bk, sltly to L, ⎮ to
	    L shldr leading ⌋ R
		S
		 Q
		 Q

4. LF bk, L shldr
    leading ss
	4. RF fwd, R shldr
	    leading ss
		S

5. RF bk in CBMP ⌉ ¼
 6. LF to side, ⎮ turn
    sltly fwd ⌋ to L
	5. LF fwd in CBMP ⌉ ¼
	 6. RF to side, ⎮ turn
	    sltly bk ⌋ to L
		Q
		 Q

7. Rf closes to LF,
    sltly bk
	7. LF closes to RF,
	    sltly fwd
		S

The natural rock turn is a forward rock turned to the right with a closed finish (steps 5, 6, 7).

A natural rock turn is used in the Taurus Tango (1991); a reverse rock turn appears in the Karen Foxtrot (1959) (but not in the 1982 dance of the same name).

Hovers

In hovers the moving or turning of the body is checked. There is elevation of the body and sway to produce a floating action. Simple hovers are often taken in an open position with feet apart and weight is transferred from one foot to the other. The hover action in these figures is often not given sufficient emphasis by sequence dancers.

In turning hovers the feet are closer together and the body turns first one way and then the other. These are very elegant movements, popular and well executed by most sequence dancers. Hovers are found in the slower dances such as slow foxtrots, waltzes and saunters. The hover cross, hover feather and hover telemark turns are standard figures in the slow foxtrot; the hover corté appears in the waltz and the quickstep.

The Hover Cross

This figure is found in many slow foxtrots. The cross action occurs on steps 4 and 5 where the left foot crosses loosely over the right foot followed by a transfer of weight to the right foot.

Hover Cross				Timing
Man's Steps		**Lady's Steps**		
1. RF fwd tng R	¼ turn to R	1. LF bk tng R	⅜ turn to R	S
2. LF to side	½ turn to R	2. RF closes to LF (heel turn)	¼ turn to R	Q
3. RF to side (pointing step)		3. LF to side		Q
4. LF fwd in CBMP OP on L side		4. RF bk in CBMP	⅛ turn to R	Q
5. Transfer wt bk to RF in CBMP	¼ turn to L	5. Transfer wt fwd to LF in CBMP OP on partner's L Side	⅛ turn to L	Q
6. LF to side, sltly fwd (pointing)		6. RF to side	⅛ tn to L	Q
7. RF fwd in CBMP OP		7. LF bk in CBMP		Q

The hover cross is found in the Amanda Foxtrot (1978), Fortuna Foxtrot (1990), Helenbrooke Waltz (1979) and Sophie Quickstep (1985). The Nicola Foxtrot (1991) has a hover cross with a rock action.

The Hover Feather

This figure has almost the same steps as the ordinary feather but a different sway and rise.

Hover Feather		Timing
Man's Steps	**Lady's Steps**	
1. LF diag fwd preparing to step OP	1. RF diag bk	Q
2. RF fwd in CBMP OP	2. LF bk in CBMP	Q

The hover feather forms part of the natural telemark, natural hover telemark and natural twist turn; it is rarely mentioned by name in sequence dance scripts. It is often taken after a pull step, e.g. after the reverse wave in the foxtrot.

The Hover Telemark

This is a telemark turn in which the dancer hovers on the second step instead of turning. It may be ended in promenade position as in the Waltz Caravelle (1967) and Rayen Waltz (1979). The Nevada Foxtrot (1990) starts with a hover telemark followed by a feather. The Emmerdale Waltz (1979) has a natural hover telemark (or promenade hover in some scripts).

Hover Telemark		Timing
Man's Steps	**Lady's Steps**	
1. LF fwd, tng L ⅛ turn 2. RF to side and LF to L brushes twd RF ⅛ 3. LF to side and turn sltly fwd (pointing) to L 4. RF fwd in CBMP OP	1. RF bk, tng L ⅛ turn 2. LF to side and RF to L brushes twd LF ⅛ 3. RF to side and turn sltly bk to L 4. LF bk in CBMP	S Q Q S

The Hover Corté

Hover Corté		Timing
Man's Steps	**Lady's Steps**	
1. RF bk, tng L ⅜ 2. LF to side, sltly fwd turn rising on toes to L (pointing step) 3. Replace wt to RF side and sltly bk	1. LF fwd, tng L ⅜ 2. RF to side, LF turn brushes twd RF to L 3. LF diag fwd	S S S

The hover corté often follows a reverse or quick open reverse turn - Caribbean Foxtrot (1986), Westmount Waltz (1989), Margie Quickstep (1990).

Turning Hovers

The hover corté is sometimes followed by a turning hover as in the Westmount Waltz (1989) and Claudia's Waltz (1991).

Claudia's Waltz (1991) and Sophie's Waltz (1993) both have a turning hover followed by a reverse pivot turn.

Other turning hovers of various types are found in the Saunter Bel-Air (1990), Callam's Waltz (1990) and the Grosvenor Foxtrot (1991).

Some special types of hover used in sequence dances are:

Forward	—	Sacha Swing (1991)
	—	Centenary Saunter (1992)
Back	—	Honeysuckle Waltz (1985)
	—	Omega Waltz (1990)
	—	Apple Blossom Waltz (1992)
Closed	—	Caribbean Foxtrot (1986)
Travelling	—	Blue Dawn Waltz (1991)
Running	—	Queslett Quickstep (1992)
Hover to PP	—	Glenroy Foxtrot (1976)
	—	Mondrago Foxtrot (1989)
	—	Westlynn Waltz (1990)
Hover from PP	—	Apple Blossom Waltz (1992)
	—	Sophie's Waltz (1993)
Hover Back Whisk	—	Waltz Cerise (1993)

In many scripts the figure is described as hover without qualification.

CHAPTER 8

WHISKS, WINGS AND ZIG-ZAGS

The Whisk

The forward whisk is essentially a triangular movement for the man ending with feet crossed; the lady turns into promenade position.

Forward Whisk		Timing	
Man's Steps	**Lady's Steps**	**W**	F
1. LF fwd	1. RF bk ⎤ ¼ turn	S	S
2. RF to side, sltly fwd	2. LF diag bk ⎦ to R	S	Q
	(pointing step)		
3. LF crosses behind RF, turning lady into PP	3. RF crosses bhd LF in PP body completes turn	S	Q

W = Waltz/F = Foxtrot

The forward whisk is often followed by a wing, e.g. Bluebird Waltz (1982), Harlequin Foxtrot (1990). Several foxtrots start with a forward whisk followed by a feather from promenade position (White Heather Foxtrot (1991), Tempro Foxtrot (1992)). The Torque Tango (1991) has a whisk following a chassé.

The Left Whisk

In this figure the man steps forward and across with the right foot. The lady usually does a **twist turn** consisting of four quick steps twisting the man to the right and allowing his feet to uncross (Bellerby Waltz (1991), Hadrian's Waltz (1992)). In the Melrose Saunter (1993) the left side whisk is followed by a same foot lunge. See also the **natural twist turn** in Chapter 10. p. 100.

Left Whisk		Waltz Timing
Man's Steps	**Lady's Steps**	
1. RF fwd and across in CBMP and PP	1. LF fwd and across in CBMP and PP ⌉ ¼ turn to L	S
2. LF to side and sltly fwd ⌉ Body turns	2. RF to side and sltly bk ⌉ ⅛	S
3. RF crosses bhd LF ⌡ L	3. LF bk in CBMP ⌡ turn to L	S

Back Whisk

Back Whisk		Timing
Man's Steps	**Lady's Steps**	
1. LF bk in CBMP	1. RF fwd in CBMP OP ⌉ ⅛ turn	S
2. RF diag bk	2. LF to side ⌡ to R	S
3. LF crosses bhd RF in PP	3. RF crosses bhd LF in PP ⌉ ⅛ turn to R	S

The Westlynn Waltz (1990) has a back whisk followed by a wing; in the Wetheral Waltz (1990) it is followed by a chassé from promenade position.

Fallaway Whisk

This is a back whisk with a turn to the right by the man also and a correspondingly larger turn by the lady.

Fallaway Whisk		Timing
Man's Steps	**Lady's Steps**	
1. LF bk ⌉ ⅜	1. RF fwd ⌉ ⅜ turn	S
2. RF to side, sltly bk (pointing step) ⌡ turn to R	2. LF to side ⌡ to R	S
		¼
3. LF crosses loosely bhd RF in fallaway	3. RF crosses loosely bhd LF in fallaway ⌉ turn ⌡ to R	S

The Emmerdale Waltz (1979) has a fallaway whisk followed by a wing; in the Misty Blues (1989) it is followed by a twist turn.

The Syncopated Whisk

Syncopated Whisk		Timing
Man's Steps	**Lady's Steps**	
1. RF fwd and across in PP and CBMP, tng R	1. LF fwd and across in PP and CBMP, tng L	S
2. LF closes to RF tng partner square	2. RF closes to LF square to partner	Q
3. RF to side ss	3. LF to side ss	Q
4. Cross LF bhd RF in PP	4. Cross RF bhd LF in PP	S

The syncopated whisk is a waltz figure usually taken from promenade position (Washington Waltz (1991)).

Two whisks are sometimes taken in succession. The Tanya Tango (1993) has a **double whisk**.

The **swivel whisk** is a figure in which the man does a type of outside swivel (see p. 106) turning the lady into whisk position. The Waltz Cerise (1993) has a **hover back whisk**.

The Wing

In the wing the man makes a small turn to the left whilst the lady walks round him to his left side.

The Wing		Timing Waltz
Man's Steps	**Lady's Steps**	
1. RF fwd and across in CBMP and PP (pointing step) — Body turns to L	1. LF fwd in CBMP and PP — 1/8 turn to L	S
2. LF starts to close to RF — 1/8 turn to L	2. RF fwd preparing to step OP — 1/4 turn to L	S
3. LF closes to RF ww — to L	3. LF fwd in CBMP OP on partner's L side — to L	S

The open telemark often follows the wing as in the Apple Blossom Waltz (1992) and Harlequin Foxtrot (1990).

The Closed Wing

This figure is similar to the normal wing but the partners are square to each other. The lady moves across the man from his right hand side to his left hand side. Closed wings with various timings occur in the Tango Las Vegas (1978), Blue Lace Waltz (1991), Cerise Saunter (1992) and April Foxtrot (1992).

Closed Wing		Timing Waltz
Man's Steps	**Lady's Steps**	
1. RF fwd in CBMP OP	1. LF bk in CBMP	S
2. LF starts to close to RF	2. RF to side, sltly bk ss	S
3. LF closes to RF ww	3. LF fwd in CBMP OP on partner's L side	S

Reverse and Natural Zig-Zag

The (reverse) zig-zag has ¼ turn to L; ¼ turn to R. The natural zig-zag has up to ¼ turn to R; ¼ turn to L although different amounts of turn are used. The 1-3 reverse zig-zag which is often found in scripts is really a quarter turn to the left. It is the 'zig' without the 'zag' - a zig-zag should turn both ways.

The (Reverse) Zig-Zag		Quick-step Timing
Man's Steps	**Lady's Steps**	
1. LF fwd ⎤ ¼ turn	1. RF bk ⎤ ¼ turn	S
2. RF to side ss ⎦ to L	2. LF closes to RF⎥ to L (heel turn) ⎦	S
3. LF bk in CBMP PO⎤ ¼	3. RF fwd in CBMP OP ⎤ ¼	S
4. Pull RF bk to LF ⎥ turn	4. LF to side ⎥ turn	S
trng on heel of LF ⎥ to	⎥ to	
5. LF fwd brushing ⎥ R	5. RF bk brushing ⎥ R	S
past RF ⎦	past LF ⎦	

The (reverse) zig-zag with various timings is found in the Woodspring Quickstep (1988), Chandella Quickstep (1990), Saunter Together (1975), Kingfisher Saunter (1990) and Tango Leanne (1992).

The **natural zig-zag** is a basic figure in the slow foxtrot; it is often taken from promenade position.

Natural Zig-Zag from Promenade Position		Timing
Man's Steps	**Lady's Steps**	
1. RF fwd and across in CBMP and PP ⎱ ⅛ turn to R 2. LF to side ⎰	1. LF fwd and across in CBMP and PP 2. RF diag fwd preparing to step OP	S S Q S
3. RF bk in CBMP ⎱ ⅛ turn to L 4. LF to side, sltly fwd (pointing step) ⎰ 5. RF fwd in CBMP OP	3. LF fwd in CBMP OP on partner's L side ⎱ ⅛ turn to L 4. RF to side ⎰ 1/8 turn to L 5. LF bk in CBMP ⎦	Q S Q S Q S

The Harlequin Foxtrot (1990), Sharron Swing (1990), Centenary Saunter (1992), Blue Lace Waltz (1991), Cameron Quickstep (1984) and Sally Ann Cha Cha Cha (1973) contain part or the whole of the natural zig-zag. Various timings are used.

The **syncopated (natural) zig-zag** (SQQS) is found in the Waltz Chambellan (1992) and Lovely Lady Waltz (1993).

The Running Zig-Zag (and Running Finish)

This quickstep figure consists of the first two steps of the zig-zag followed by the running finish. The Idaho Foxtrot (1959) has a reverse running zig-zag; the Claymore Cha Cha Cha (1991) has both natural and reverse running zig-zags.

The **running finish** is used in many sequence quicksteps. In the Quando Quickstep and Roxy Quickstep (1991) it follows a back lock and leads into a natural spin turn. In the Florentine Quickstep (1992), the alternative timing SQQS is used.

Running Zig-Zag (Reverse)			Quick-step Timing
	Man's Steps	Lady's Steps	
Zig-Zag	1. LF fwd ⎤ ¼ turn to L 2. RF to side, slitly bk ss ⎦	1. RF bk ⎤ ¼ turn to L 2. LF closes to RF (heel turn) ⎦	S S
Run. Fin.	3. LF bk in CBMP ldg ptnr outside ⎤ ¼ turn to R 4. RF to side ⎦ 5. LF diag fwd, L shldr ldg preparing to step OP 6. RF fwd in CBMP OP	3. RF fwd in CBMP OP ⎤ ¼ turn to R 4. LF to side ⎦ 5. RF diag bk, R shldr ldg 6. LF bk in CBMP PO	Q Q S S

Zig-Zag Back Lock and Running Finish

This is a standard figure in the quickstep preferred by many ballroom dancers to the running zig-zag. It is found in the Roxy Quickstep (1991) and Quality Quickstep (1992).

Zig-Zag, Back Lock, Running Finish		Timing
Man's Steps	Lady's Steps	
1. LF fwd tng L ⎤ ¼ turn to L	1. RF bk tng L ⎤ ⅜ turn to L	S
2. RF to side ⎦ ⎤ ⅛ turn to L	2. LF closes to RF ⎦ (heel turn)	S
3. LF bk in CBMP ⎦	3. RF fwd in CBMP OP	S
4. RF bk	4. LF diag fwd	Q
5. LF crosses in front of RF	5. RF crosses bhd LF	Q
6. RF diag bk	6. LF diag fwd	S
7. LF bk in CBMP tng R ⎤ ⅜ turn to R	7. RF fwd in CBMP OP tng R ⎤ ¼ turn to R	Q
8. RF to side, sltly fwd (pointing step) ⎦	8. LF to side ⎦ ⎤ ⅛ turn to R	Q
9. LF fwd, L shldr ldg, prepg to step OP	9. RF bk, R shldr leading ⎦	S
10. RF fwd in CBMP OP	10. LF bk in CBMP	S

The Four Step and Turning Four Step

The **four step** is a standard figure in the tango. Four steps occur in the Evening Foxtrot (1984), Tango Debonaire (1990), Carousel Saunter (1991) and Cheney Blues (1992).

Tango Four Step		Tango Timing
Man's Steps	**Lady's Steps**	
1. LF fwd in CBMP	1. RF bk in CBMP	Q
2. RF to side, sltly bk	2. LF to side, sltly fwd	Q
3. LF bk in CBMP	3. RF fwd in CBMP OP ⎤ ¼	Q
4. RF closes to LF,	4. LF closes to RF, ⎟ turn	Q
sltly bk in PP	sltly bk in PP ⎦ to R	

The **turning four step**, which is the tango four step with a turn to the left has its first three steps very similar to steps 1-3 of the reverse zig-zag. It is found in the Saunter Sateen (1991), Tango Leanne (1992), Starlight Gavotte (1993) and Harvestime Blues (1989).

The Four Step Change (or Habanera)

Like the change in direction in foxtrot and quickstep, this is used to change the direction of travel in the tango. It is a turning four step with a ¼ turn to the left on steps 1 and 2 followed by:- Step 3. LF closes to RF; Step 4. RF back (very small step). The Tango Givenchy (1986) has a four step change; the Red Rose Tango (1963) has a close to a Habanera.

Five Steps

These are turning four steps with an extra backward step followed by a movement into promenade position. There are varying amounts of turn and they may be taken from different alignments. The sharp turn to the promenade position on the last step is sometimes called a **switch**. A switch is mentioned in the Suhali Tango (1970) and also in the Waikiki Cha Cha Cha (1993).

The Tango Vienna (1993) has a **mini five step**; the Lancaster Tango (1987) and Tango Danielle (1993) have **five step turns**.

87

The Reverse Wave

This is a standard figure in the slow foxtrot; it is a type of zig-zag with a turn to the left followed by a turn to the right.

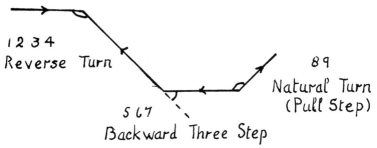

1 2 3 4
Reverse Turn

5 6 7
Backward Three Step

8 9
Natural Turn
(Pull Step)

Steps 1 2 3 4   Forward half of open reverse turn (3/8L), see page 98

Steps 5 6 7   Curving backward three step (1/8L)

Steps 8 9   Pull step - steps 5, 6 of open natural turn (3/8R), see page 98

The reverse wave is found in the Ellis Foxtrot (1989) and Stardust Foxtrot (1993); many foxtrots have only some steps of the wave, e.g. Glenroy Foxtrot (1976), Evening Foxtrot (1984).

The Extended Reverse Wave

This is one of the newer ballroom dancing figures. A back feather and curving three step are introduced after the normal backward curving three step in the reverse wave making 15 steps in all. This figure involves a remarkably long progression against the line of dance and seems particularly suited to sequence slow foxtrots.

CHAPTER 9

CHASSÉS, QUARTER TURNS AND LOCK STEPS

A chassé (chasing step) consists essentially of three steps counted Quick, Quick, Slow with the feet being closed on the second step. Like the three-step of the slow foxtrot it changes the rhythm and the leading foot. Many chassés are taken in a sideways or diagonal direction.

Side Chassés

Chassé to R	Chassé to L	Timing
Man's Steps	Man's Steps	
1. RF to side 2. LF closes to RF 3. RF to side	1. LF to side 2. RF closes to LF 3. LF to side	Q Q S
————————> Often written as chassé RLR	<———————— Often written as chassé LRL	

(The lady does the opposite side chassé to the man.) The short form of notation for the chassé is used in some dance scripts, e.g.

Anitra Cha Cha Cha (Bar 1)
> Side LF to chassé LRL

Cuban Swing (Bar 5)
> Chassé LRL towards centre

Chassé figures are common in the quickstep, cha cha cha and jive. In the cha cha cha and jive the feet are only half-closed on the second step. The jive chassé has a timing of $3/4, 1/4, 1$ instead of $1/2, 1/2, 1$ (QQS) as in the other dances.

Many lock steps are alternatives to the chassé in which one foot is crossed behind the other instead of the feet being closed on the second step. Forward chassés are often replaced by lock steps.

The chassé is often preceded by a walking (slow) step and many chassés are of the form:-

S Q Q S

Feet closed

The nature and direction of these two slow steps determine the character of the chassé dancing figure. If there is no turn within the chassé itself the lady's steps are opposite to the man's and the figures are easy to describe and execute.

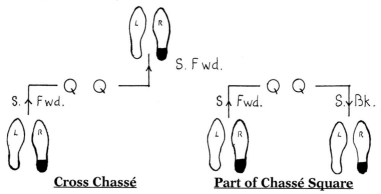

Cross Chassé   **Part of Chassé Square**

Notice that the feet are always pointing in the same direction although the legs move forwards, backwards and sideways.

Cross Chassés

Cross Chassé to R	Timing
Man's steps; lady's are opposite	
1. LF fwd	S
2. RF to side	Q
3. LF closes to RF	Q

This is a triangular figure like the closed change in the waltz. It is usually followed by a step with the right foot outside the partner.

Chassé Squares

Chassé squares are common in older sequence dances. Waltz squares have similar steps but different timing (no chassé).

Clockwise Chassé Square	Timing	
Man's Steps	Chassé	Waltz
1. LF fwd	S	S
2. RF to side	Q	S
3. LF closes to RF	Q	S
4. RF bk	S	S
5. LF to side	Q	S
6. RF closes to LF	Q	S

(Lady's steps are opposite)

Examples of sequence dances using chassé squares appear in Chapter 2, p. 35.

Promenade Chassés

Partners carry out the chassés moving down the line of dance in promenade position. The feet and body are diagonal to the direction of motion. The Apple Blossom Waltz (1992) has this figure in bars 2 and 13. The promenade chassé or 'conversation piece' is a standard figure in social rhythm dancing.

Promenade Chassé	Timing
Man's steps; lady's steps are opposite	
1. RF fwd and across in CBMP and PP	S
2. LF to side and sltly fwd in PP	Q
3. RF closes to LF in PP	Q
4. LF to side and sltly fwd	S

Chassé Quarter Turns

The four chassé quarter turns are standard figures in the quickstep. They are forward and backward chassés turning both to right and to left; they are often taken down the line of dance.

Forward Chassés

1. Quarter Turn to Right

2. Progressive Chassé to Right (really a quarter turn to the left)

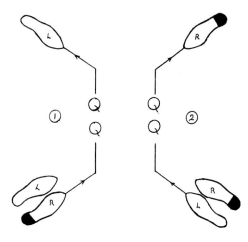

Backward Chassés

3. Tipple chassé

4. Progressive chassé

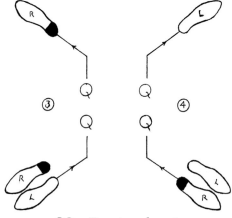

QQ = Turning chassé

The Chassé Quarter Turns						
		Man's Steps				Turn
		1	2	3	4	
1	Quarter Turn to R	RF fwd	LF to side	RF closes to LF	LF to side sltly bk	⅛ R over 1,2 ⅛ R over 2,3
2	Progressive Chassé to R	LF fwd	RF to side	LF closes to RF	RF to side sltly bk	⅛ L over 1,2 ⅛ L over 2,3
3	Tipple Chassé	LF bk	RF to side	LF closes to RF	RF to side sltly fwd	¼ R over 1,2
4	Progressive Chassé	RF bk	LF to side	RF closes to LF	LF to side sltly fwd	¼ L over 1,2
	Timing	S	Q	Q	S	

Lady's steps for (2) are (4); for (1) are (3) and vice versa.

Notice that in (1) and (2) the man is moving **forward** on the **outside** of the turn; the turn takes place over all three steps. In (3) and (4) he is moving **backward** on the **inside** of the turn and turns on the first two steps.

The Florentine Quickstep (1992) starts with a single change step followed by a quarter turn to the right. The Eivona Quickstep (1974) starts with a progressive chassé to the right and has double tipple chassés and double progressive chassés. Progressive chassés are common in waltzes.

Dances Starting with 123 ReverseTurn, Progressive Chassé

Many modern sequence waltzes and quicksteps start with these figures using a SSS timing for the waltz reverse turn and a chassé QQS timing for the quickstep reverse turn. The progressive chassé has now become a very popular ending to the reverse turn. It is nearly always followed by a natural figure starting with a right foot step outside partner.

Dance		Figure which follows the Reverse Turn and Progressive Chassé
Cameron Quickstep	(1984)	Forward Lock Step
Quatro Quickstep	(1991)	Natural Turn
Linden Swing	(1992)	Promenade Lock
Waltz Daniella	(1976)	Natural Turn
Wensley Waltz	(1990)	Curved Feather
Denverdale Waltz	(1992)	Natural Spin Turn
Waltz Cerise	(1993)	Curved Feather

The corresponding figures in the opposite direction are the 123 Natural Turn followed by the Tipple Chassé. These two figures are found in the Universal Quickstep (1967), Waltz Daniella (1976), Kontiki Quickstep (1986).

The chassé quarter turns are often overturned to $\frac{3}{8}$ as in the Quatro Quickstep (1991) or underturned to $\frac{1}{8}$.

The Naming of Quarter Turns

The quarter turn to the right has a body turn to the right with the man's chassé to the left - it is named by body turn.

The progressive chassé to the right has a left body turn with the man's chassé to the right. It is named by direction of foot movement in the chassé and is really a quarter turn to the left.

The tipple chassé is described in some scripts as chassé R or even progressive chassé R. It has a right body turn and a man's chassé to the right. (The progressive chassé has both movements to the left.) 'Tipple chassé' is sometimes used to indicate a side chassé with a sway - Waltz Clinique (1991), Blue Dawn Waltz (1991).

These names have arisen from history but are confusing for the beginner.

Quarter Turn to the Left

The full **quickstep quarter turn** is a zig-zag movement consisting of a quarter turn first to right and then to left. The turn to the right is the **quarter turn to the right** just considered. The left turn can be achieved in two ways by:-

(a) **The Progressive Chassé** - the backward chassé left quarter turn just dealt with; this is used if the following figure is a natural turn or a step outside partner; or,

(b) The Quarter Turn to the Left - this is the standard figure described in the ballroom dancing manuals.

Quarter Turn to Left					Timing
	Man's Steps		**Lady's Steps**		
Heel pivot	1. RF bk	¼ turn to L	1. LF fwd	⅛ turn to L	S
	2. LF starts to close to RF		2. RF to side		Q
	3. LF closes to RF ww		3. LF closes to RF	⅛ turn to L	Q
	4. LF fwd		4. RF bk		S

This figure is the progressive chassé (considered earlier) with the man's chassé replaced by a **heel pivot** - this is a turn on the heel of one foot without any transfer of weight. The heel pivot is performed by the man while the lady does a chassé and is found only in the quickstep. It is neater than a small chassé and is a type of hesitation, two movements being taken with the same working foot.

The Maestro Quickstep (1983) and Florentine Quickstep (1992) finish with the quarter turn to the left.

Forward and Backward Lock Steps

A lock step is a type of chassé in which one foot is crossed behind the other instead of being closed on the third step. Lock steps are often used instead of the chassés.

Forward Lock Step	Backward Lock Step	Timing
Man's or Lady's Steps	Man's or Lady's Steps	
1. RF fwd in CBMP OP	1. LF bk in CBMP	S
2. LF fwd sltly to L	2. RF bk	Q
3. RF crosses bhd LF	3. LF crosses in front of RF	Q
4. LF fwd sltly to L	4. RF bk sltly to R	S

A **turning back lock** is a backward lock step followed by a quarter turn to the left on the following step; it often follows the natural spin turn in the waltz.

The Chandella Quickstep (1990) and Nicola Foxtrot (1991) have double forward locks whereas the Quatro Quickstep (1991) has a double backward lock. Hadrian's Waltz (1992) has a back lock and a slow lock; the slow lock step is not a chasse.

The Fishtail

This is a popular figure in sequence quicksteps, e.g. Universal Quickstep (1967), Quando Quickstep (1979); it is found also in the Singapore Swing (1992).

Fishtail		Timing
Man's steps; lady's steps are opposite		
Lock on opp. foot	1. RF fwd in CBMP OP	S
	2. LF crosses behind RF	Q
	3. RF fwd sltly to side, ss	Q
Lock on normal foot	4. LF fwd sltly to L, L shldr ldg	Q
	5. RF crosses behind LF	Q
	6. LF fwd sltly to L	S

The fishtail may be danced without turn or there may be ¼ turn to the right between steps 1 and 3. There is a sway to the right on 2 and to the left on 4 which gives the fishtail its name. A back fishtail is found in the Queslett Quickstep (1992).

CHAPTER 10

DANCING TURNS

Closed and Open Turns

A **closed turn** may be a turn in which the feet are closed at some stage, e.g. the third and sixth steps of the waltz turn. In the **open turn** the feet pass one another instead of closing as in the foxtrot reverse turn.

The **closed turn** may, however, be a turn with a **closed finish** - finishing square to partner. In the closed telemark turn the feet are **not** closed on any of the three steps. The **open turn** may be a turn finishing in open position, e.g promenade position. The open impetus turn in the waltz has the feet **closed** on the second step.

Forward and Backward Turns

Many turns used in sequence dances can be divided into a forward (123) and a backward (456) movement. The forward part of one turn is often followed by the backward part of another figure. Instead of closing or passing, the feet may cross on the third step. In the basic tango reverse turn and reverse cross the man's foot crosses in front, in the twist turns it crosses behind.

Heel Turns

Steps must be shorter when moving backwards on the inside of a turn and in some cases a **heel turn** is used. As the backward foot is turning, the other foot is closed to it in parallel position and weight transferred. Examples are lady's step 2 in the open natural and reverse turns in the foxtrot and in the zig-zag. A man's heel turn occurs on step 2 of the impetus turn. A **heel pull** or **pull step** is a heel turn in which the feet remain apart at the end of the turn - it is a stronger step taken with the weight of the body more forward. Examples of the heel pull are man's step 5 in the open natural turn in the foxtrot and the hesitation change in the waltz.

Open Turns

The man's feet do not close at any stage in the foxtrot natural turn. The man's steps consist of an open turn followed by a heel pull; the lady does a heel turn, a turning three step and a brush step.

Open Natural Turn		Timing
Man's Steps	**Lady's Steps**	
1. RF fwd ⎤ ¼ turn to R 2. LF to side ⎦ 　　　⎤ ⅛ turn 　　　⎥ to R 3. RF bk ⎦ 4. LF bk ⎤ ⅜ turn 5. RF to side ss ⎥ to R 　(a heel pull) ⎦ 6. LF fwd	1. LF bk ⎤ ⅜ turn 2. RF closes to LF⎦ to R 　(heel turn) 3. LF fwd 4. RF fwd ⎤ ⅜ turn 5. LF to side and ⎦ to R 　RF brushes twd LF 6. RF bk	S Q Q S S S

Open turns are found in the Cameron Quickstep (1984), Washington Waltz (1991) and Philishar Foxtrot (1993).

Open Reverse Turn		Timing
Man's Steps	**Lady's Steps**	**Foxtrot**
1. LF fwd ⎤ ¼ turn to L 2. RF to side⎦ ⎤ ⅛ turn 3. LF bk ⎦ to L 4. RF bk ⎤ ⅜ turn 5. LF to side, ⎥ to L 　sltly fwd ⎦ 6. RF fwd in CBMP OP	1. RF bk ⎤ ⅜ turn 2. LF closes to RF⎦ to L 3. RF fwd (heel turn) 4. LF fwd ⎤ ¼ turn to L 5. RF to side ⎦ ⎤ 　　　⎥ ⅛ turn 6. LF bk in CBMP⎦ to L	S Q Q S Q Q

In this foxtrot open reverse turn the man walks round without closing whilst the lady does a heel turn on step 2. Steps 4-6 are sometimes called a 'feather finish'. The Iris Foxtrot (1964) and Nicola Foxtrot (1991) have the complete open reverse turn. The Saunter Shakara (1992) has the 1-3 open reverse turn and the 4-6 open reverse turn later.

The **open reverse turn with open finish** in the tango is a similar turn with a different timing. The Torque Tango (1991) and Saunter Sateen (1991) have this figure.

The Quick Open Reverse Turn

This is an open reverse turn danced to a quicker rhythm with the lady outside on the third step (Quatro Quickstep (1991), Sheridan Waltz (1990)).

Quick Open Reverse				Timing
Man's Steps		**Lady's Steps**		**Quickstep**
1. LF fwd	¼ turn	1. RF bk	⅜ turn	S
2. RF to side	to L	2. LF to side,	to L	Q
	⅛ turn	sltly fwd		
3. LF bk in CBMP	to L	3. RF fwd in CBMP OP		Q

The **weave** is a type of open reverse turn often taken from promenade position. It is used in the Waltz Clinique (1991) and Grosvenor Foxtrot (1991). The Waltz Cerise (1993) has a **syncopated reverse weave**. The **natural weave** has the same ending as the weave but turns first right and then left. It is a type of zig-zag figure used in foxtrots, e.g. Harlequin Foxtrot (1990).

The Basic Reverse Tango Turn

Basic Reverse Tango Turn				Timing
Man's Steps		**Lady's Steps**		
1. LF fwd in CBMP		1. RF bk in CBMP		Q
2. RF to side, sltly bk		2. LF to side, sltly fwd		Q
3. LF crosses in front of RF	¾ turn	3. RF closes to LF, sltly bk	¾ turn	S
4. RF bk	to	4. LF fwd	to	Q
5. LF to side, sltly fwd	L	5. RF to side, sltly bk	L	Q
6. RF closes to LF, sltly bk		6. LF closes to RF, sltly fwd		S

The basic tango reverse turn with an open finish is found in the Telecon and Trafalgar Tangos (1992).

Steps 2 and 3 are known as the **reverse cross**. This is found in Claudia's Waltz (1991), Saunter St. Clair (1992). The Waltz Clinique (1991) has a double cross; this is called a back lock and a slow lock in Hadrian's Waltz (1992).

The opposite figure is the **cross** which is:- Step 2. LF to side, sltly bk; Step 3. RF crosses behind LF. This is found in the Waltz Chambellan (1992) and Tango Torviscas (1992). The Tanya Tango (1993) has a reverse pivot followed by a cross.

The Natural Twist Turn

This is closely related to the left whisk (see Chapter 8, page 81). In the standard figures in the foxtrot and tango, the three whisk steps are included in the turn - in sequences it is often referred to as left whisk, twist turn. The man steps forward with his right foot, then to side with his left foot, then crosses his right foot behind his left foot. The lady then runs round the man to untwist his feet. There is a turn to right of between $\frac{3}{8}$ and a full turn with various timings. It is taken in open position in the tango and saunter and in closed position in the foxtrot and waltz.

The left whisk is followed by a twist turn in Callam's Waltz (1990) and a fallaway twist turn in the Suhali Tango (1970) and Telecon Tango (1992); by an untwist to PP in the Centenary Saunter (1992).

In Sophie's Waltz (1993) the twist turn follows a natural spin turn; in the Misty Blues (1989) it follows a fallaway whisk.

The Natural Promenade Turn

This is a favourite turn in the tango. It is started and finished in promenade position with a turn of $\frac{3}{4}$ to the right; the man just steps round taking the lady with him. It is found in the Newfield Tango (1990), Tango Vilamoura (1990), Saunter Simone (1989), Saunter Sateen (1991) and Stephanne Blues (1993).

The Natural Spin Turn

Natural Spin Turn		Timing	
Man's Steps	**Lady's Steps**	**W**	**Q**
1-3 Natural Turn	1-3 Natural Turn	SSS	SQQ
4. LF bk, RF ⌉ ½ turn to R held in CBMP	4. RF fwd ⌉ ½ turn to R (pivoting action)	S	S
5. RF fwd ⌉ ⅜	5. LF bk, sltly to L ⌉ ⅜	S	S
6. LF to side, │ turn sltly bk ⌡ to R	6. RF diag fwd │ turn having brushed │ to to LF ⌡ R	S	S

W=Waltz/Q=Quickstep

Step 4 is the **pivot** which is a turn on the ball of one foot in which the other foot is kept in front after a backward step in CBMP. Steps 5 and 6 are the **spin**. The spin turn is very popular in both the waltz and the quickstep. The Katrina Quickstep (1992) has steps 4 to 6 following a curved feather.

Natural and Reverse Pivot Turns

The **natural pivot turn** is steps 1 to 4 of the spin turn - the natural turn followed by the pivot. Natural pivots are found in the Iris Foxtrot (1964) and Washington Waltz (1991). The Florentine Quickstep (1992) has a reverse pivot. Claudia's Waltz (1991) and Sophie's Waltz (1993) have a reverse pivot following a turning hover. The **slip pivot** is the usual way in which the lady turns from fallaway position or chair to square with partner. She turns strongly on the ball of the right foot to the left to face her partner and then slips her foot between the partner's continuing to turn. It is really two pivots:

1. RF bk in CBMP and fallaway turning strongly left - a small step with LF held in CBMP.

2. LF fwd in CBMP with RF behind held in CBMP still turning.

Slip pivots may involve ¾ or more turn to the left. They are found in the Westlynn Waltz (1990), Felicity Foxtrot (1990) and Saunter Solazur (1992).

The Impetus Turn

Impetus Turn		Timing		
Man's Steps	**Lady's Steps**	**F**	**W**	**Q**
1-3 Natural Turn	1-3 Natural Turn	SQQ	SSS	SQQ
4. LF bk ⎤ 3/8 turn	4. RF fwd ⎤ 3/8 turn	S	S	S
5. RF closes to ⎦ to R	5. LF to side ⎦ to R	Q	S	S
LF ⎦ 1/4	1/4			
6. LF to side, turn	6. RF diag fwd turn	Q	S	S
sltly bk ⎦ to R	having ⎦ to R			
	brushed to LF			

F=Foxtrot/W=Waltz/Q=Quickstep. Man's steps 4 and 5 are a heel turn.

The (closed) impetus turn can be seen as an alternative to the spin turn. The White Heather Foxtrot (1991) has 4 to 6 of the impetus turn with a feather ending; the Blue Lace Waltz (1991) has the same figure described as with an open finish. The **open impetus turn** has step 6 replaced by a diagonal forward step into promenade position; the lady moves to the side in promenade position after a brush step. The Waltz Clinique (1991) has a full open impetus turn, the Queslett Quickstep (1992) has steps 4 to 6 followed by a lock step.

The Reverse Corté

In some respects the first three steps of the reverse corté may be seen as the opposite to the impetus turn with a turn to the left instead of the right.

1 to 3 Reverse Corté		Timing
Man's Steps	**Lady's Steps**	
1. RF bk ⎤ 3/8 turn	1. LF fwd ⎤ 1/4 turn to L	S
2. LF closes to RF ⎦ to L	2. RF to side ⎦	S
ww ⎦	1/8 turn	
3. Position held	3.LF closes to RF ⎦ to L	S

The Bluebird Waltz (1982) and Apple Blossom Waltz (1992) have 1 to 3 of the reverse turn followed by the 1 to 3 of the reverse corté.

Telemark Turns

The name 'telemark' is taken from a swing turn in skiing. The legs are stepped round rather than swung as in waltz turns. Telemark turns are compact turns through a large angle used with great effect in the slow foxtrot; they are also standard figures in the waltz and the quickstep.

Closed Telemark		Timing	
Man's Steps	**Lady's Steps**	**W**	**F**
1. LF fwd ⌉ ⅜ turn	1. RF bk ⌉⅜ turn	S	S
2. RF to side ⌋ to L	2. LF closes to RF⌋ ⌉ to L	S	Q
3. LF to side, ⅜ turn	3. RF to side, ⅜ turn	S	Q
sltly fwd ⌋ to L	sltly bk ⌋ to L		

W = Waltz/F = Foxtrot. The lady's second step is a heel turn.

The April Foxtrot (1992) has a telemark turn followed by a feather step. The Waltz Wynette (1985) has a telemark followed by a 1 to 3 natural turn. In the Appleby and Chandella Quicksteps (1990) they are called closed telemarks.

The **open telemark** is a telemark turn finished in promenade position; the man turns more than the lady.

Open Telemark		Timing	
Man's Steps	**Lady's Steps**	**W**	**F**
1. LF fwd ⌉ ¼ turn	1. RF bk ⌉⅜ turn	S	S
2. RF to side ⌋ to L	2. LF closes to RF⌋ to L	S	Q
3. LF to side, ½ turn	3. RF diag fwd in	S	Q
in PP ⌋ to L	PP, R shldr ldg		

W = Waltz/F = Foxtrot. The lady's second step is a heel turn.

The Woodside Waltz (1964), Emmerdale Waltz (1979) and the Apple Blossom Waltz (1992) all have open telemark turns followed by a hover from promenade position and a contra check. The White Heather Foxtrot (1991) and the Tempro Foxtrot (1992) both have an open telemark followed by 1 to 3 of the open natural turn. There is an open telemark in the Tango Torviscas (1992).

The natural telemark involves a ¾ turn to the right with a feather-type ending, e.g. Wetheral Waltz (1990), Harlequin Foxtrot (1990).

Natural Telemark		Timing
Man's Steps	**Lady's Steps**	

1. RF fwd   ¼ turn
2. LF to side   to R
       ½ turn
3. RF to side ss   to R
 	
4. LF diag fwd,
     L shldr ldg
5. RF fwd in CBMP OP
	1. LF bk ⅜ turn
	2. RF closes to LF to R
	     (heel turn) ⅜ turn
	3. LF to side, to R
	     RF brushes to LF
	4. RF diag bk,
	     R shldr ldg
	5. LF bk in CBMP
		S
		Q
		
		Q
		
		Q
		
		Q

The Top Spin

Top Spin		Timing
Man's Steps	**Lady's Steps**	

1. LF bk in CBMP   ¼ turn
2. RF bk   to L
3. LF to side,   ¼ turn
     sltly fwd   to L
4. RF fwd in CBMP OP
	1. RF fwd in CBMP OP ¼ turn
	2. LF fwd to L
	3. RF to side ¼
	       turn
	4. LF bk in CBMP to L
		Q
		Q
		Q
		
		Q

The Nevada Foxtrot (1990) and the White Heather Foxtrot (1991) both end with an impetus turn and feather ending followed by a top spin. The Waltz Rabanne (1992) has a top spin following a closed impetus turn.

Double Reverse Spin

Double Reverse Spin		Timing
Man's Steps	**Lady's Steps**	
1. LF fwd ⎤ ⅜ turn to L 2. RF to side ⎦ ⎤ ½ 3. LF closes to RF ww ⎮ turn (Toe Pivot) ⎦ to L	1. RF bk ⎤ ½ turn to L 2. LF closes to RF ⎦⎤ ¼ turn 3. RF to side, ⎤ to L sltly bk ⎦ ⅛ 4. LF crosses in front ⎮ turn of RF ⎦ to L	S S Q S S

The lady's second step is a heel turn. She does four steps to three beats while the man does three steps. This figure is not really a spin and there is no need to dance it twice. Double reverse spins are found in William's Waltz (1985), the Kirsty Quickstep (1989) and the Nicola Foxtrot (1991).

The Outside Spin

Outside Spin		Timing
Man's Steps	**Lady's Steps**	
1. LF bk in CBMP ⎤ ⅜ turn (small step) ⎦ to R 2. RF fwd in CBMP OP ⎤ ⅜ 3. LF to side, ⎮ turn turning ¼ to R ⎮ to end with LF back ⎦ R	1. RF fwd in CBMP ⎤ ⅝ turn OP ⎦ to R 2. LF closes to RF ⎤ ¼ 3. RF fwd between ⎮ turn partner's feet ⎮ to R turning ⅛ to R ⎦	S S S

There is a gradual whole turn to the right throughout the figure. The Fortuna Foxtrot (1990), Callam's Waltz (1990) and Hadrian's Waltz (1992) have outside spins.

Swivels

A swivel involves a turning of the body (and feet) without progression along the line of dance. It may be taken on the toe or the ball or foot. The feet may be together as in the swivels in the rotary turn or apart as in the swivel turn.

The **outside swivel** is a popular figure in the tango, foxtrot and other dances.

Outside Swivel			Timing
Man's Steps		**Lady's Steps**	
1. LF bk in CBMP ⌉ ¼ 　 RF crosses in front ⎮ turn 　 of LF ww to end ⎮ to 　 in PP ⌋ R		1. RF fwd in CBMP OP ⌉ ½ 　 and LF closes to RF ⎮ turn 　 sltly bk ww to end ⎮ to 　 in PP ⌋ R	S
2. RF fwd and across in 　 CBMP and PP		2. LF fwd and across in 　 CBMP and PP starting 　 to turn L	S

Step 1 is the swivel.

A popular sequence in the foxtrot is the open telemark, natural turn outside swivel, e.g. Glenroy Foxtrot (1976) and Nevada Foxtrot (1990).

In tangos the outside swivel is often followed by steps 2 and 3 of the promenade link (Torque Tango (1991), Tango Torviscas (1992)). The Merrick Tango (1993) has a double outside swivel. Outside swivels occur in the Saunter Si Bon (1985), Centenery Saunter (1992) and Washington Waltz (1991).

The **cross swivel** is a standard figure in the quickstep. The man takes a long step with his left foot and closes the right foot to it (slightly back) without weight turning ¼ to the left. It is found in the Cresta Quickstep (1988).

There are many other swivel steps:-

Side swivels	-	Kontiki Quickstep (1986)
Backward swivels	-	Grosvenor Foxtrot (1991)
Hesitation swivels	-	Denverdale Waltz (1992)
Swivels left and right	-	Saunter St. Clair (1992)
Lock, step and swivel	-	Cheney Blues (1992)
Walk Point and Swivel	-	Sacha Swing (1991)

CHAPTER 11

THE RUMBA AND CHA CHA CHA

Although the cha cha cha and rumba are very different in character they have many similarities. Thus both dances are written in 4/4 time and should be started on the second beat. In many figures the cha cha cha chassé is replaced by a single slow step in the rumba. The standard rhythms of the two dances are set out below.

Script Timing	Cha Cha Cha					Rumba		
	2	**3**	**4**	**and**	**1**	**2**	**3**	**4 1**
Beat values	1	1	½	½	1	1	1	2
	Step	Step	Cha	Cha	Cha			
	S	S	Q	Q	S	Q	Q	S
				Chassé				

Notice that the slow step takes 1 beat in the cha cha cha but 2 beats in the rumba. Hence timings in this section will be given in beat values. Compare the forward figures for the two dances.

Forward Basic				
Man's steps; lady's steps are opposite				
	Cha Cha Cha	**Beat Values**	**Rumba**	**Beat Values**
Chassé LRL	1. LF fwd	1	1. LF fwd	1
	2. Replace wt to RF	1	2. Replace wt to RF	1
	3. LF to side, sltly bk	½		
	4. RF half closed to LF	½	3. LF to side	2
	5. LF to side	1		
	⅛ - ¼ turn to L		⅛ - ¼ turn to L	

The steps of the back basic are similar but starting with right foot back for the man followed by a RLR chassé.

The Rumba and the Cha Cha Cha Compared

The ballroom **rumba** is sometimes called the single beat mambo (the cha cha cha is the triple beat or Cuban mambo). Sequence rumbas are played at 26-32 bpm and their timing is invariably 2 3 4.1 best remembered as Quick, Quick, Slow (Q = 1, S = 2 beats). The rumba is a gay exotic sensual dance with a characteristic smooth supple hip movement produced by alternately flexing and stretching the knees. Small steps are taken placing the feet firmly on the floor. Steps are taken first on the toe followed by the ball of the foot and finally the heel (this type of footwork is described as ball-flat) - heel leads are not used in the rumba.

The **cha cha cha** is played at 31-33 bpm and its basic rhythm is 2 3 4 and 1, commonly called Step, Step, Cha Cha Cha (SSQQS). Another rhythm used is 2 and 3, 4 and 1 (QQSQQS) and dances sometimes end with 2 3 4 1 (SSSS) (Q = $\frac{1}{2}$, S = 1 beat). The cha cha cha has a compulsive staccato rhythm and is danced very much on the beat - it is not a smooth, flowing dance like the rumba. Steps are very precise and the footwork is ball-flat; the hip movements are more definite than in the rumba but not to the extent of bouncing up and down. Unlike the modern dances there are many holds and positions and the dancers have much freedom of action. Walter Laird lists 23 basic positions for starting or ending the dancing figures. There may be:-

No hand hold	-	solo turns, Cuban break, change of place
One hand hold	-	opposite hands (LH-RH) or same hands, e.g. RH-RH (handshake hold)
Double hand hold	-	opposite hands (LH-RH) as in parallel facing position or cuddle hold
	-	same hands as in skating hold or some forms of shadow hold (LH-LH; RH-RH)

If there is a free hand it should be moved about gracefully to complement the body motion without being conspicuous. General rules are not easy to formulate - it is best to watch the experts but resist the tendency to overdo the movements.

Basic Positions

(a) Facing holds

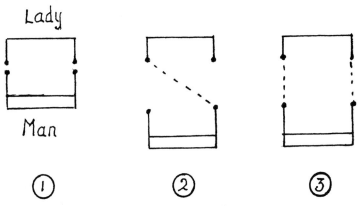

Close facing position (1) is similar in many respects to ballroom hold with light body contact; in **closed facing position** the partners are about 6" apart.

Open facing positions have the dancers more or less at arms length. (2) is handshake hold, (3) is double hold in parallel position. There may be no hold, a single hold with opposite hands or a crossed arm double hold.

(b) Side-by-side holds

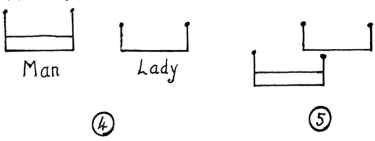

Diagram (4) represents **right side-by-side position**; **left side-by-side position** has the lady on the left. In **shadow hold** (5) left hands are held with the man's right hand on the lady's shoulder blade; sometimes the right hands are held as well as left hands. In **cuddle hold** opposite hands are held with the man's right arm round the lady's waist.

(c) V-shaped holds

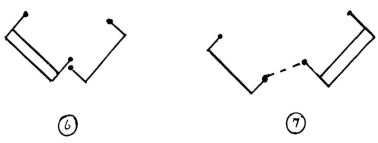

Promenade position is (6); counter promenade position has the lady on the left. **Fallaway position** is obtained by taking one pace backwards from promenade position with an outward turn of ⅛. The **aida** reaches a similar position by taking 3 steps back from close facing position and turning by ⅜. The **fan** is position (7) - the lady's right hand is held in the man's left hand.

Solo Turns

These are turning basics without hand hold and may be taken to right or to left. There are 3 circling walks in the rumba, 2 walks and a chassé in the cha cha cha. They may be spot turns or involve travel down the line of dance.

Underarm Turns

The **alemana** (allemande) is a turn by the lady under the man's raised arm and is found in tangos and many old-time dances. In rumbas and cha cha chas it is usually a turn to the **right** under the man's left arm (lady's RH in man's LH). If it is started in fan position and ended in facing position, the total turn is 1⅛. The **Turkish Towel** starts with an alemana in handshake hold - the man turns the lady under his right arm and moves across in front of her towards the wall then back to centre, then back to wall. He has his back to the lady for these turns like rubbing the back with a long towel.

110

The **hockey stick** involves the lady taking 3 steps across the man before turning **left** under the man's raised left arm (Lady's RH in mans's LH). From fan position to facing position the lady's turn is $\frac{5}{8}$ (shape of a hockey stick).

The **spiral** is another **left** turn for the lady in which she crosses her feet (spiral cross).

In **rope spinning** the man goes underneath the raised arms while the lady walks round him - he may or may not turn himself (like a man spinning a lasso round his body). Lakeside Rumba (1991), Katie Cha Cha (1993).

The Natural Top

After a basic movement towards the wall the man moves into close facing position and starts to turn **right** by crossing his right foot behind his left foot and taking a left foot step to the side ($\frac{1}{4}$ turn). He continues to repeat these steps until the desired amount of turn has been achieved. This is a popular figure in both the rumba and the cha cha cha.

The Reverse Top

This is the opposite turn to the natural top in which there is a turn to the left with the man's left foot crossing **in front of** his right foot, e.g. Venezia Rumba (1993). Richard's Rumba (1992) has a continuous hip twist with the left foot crossing **behind**. These reverse turns are not easy to perform well and are rarely found in sequence dances.

The Anitra Cha Cha Cha (1991) has a reverse turn with some chassés and crossing of feet - the figures are described as cross basics.

Figures with Checks

In the checking action weight is transferred to the leading foot and then replaced to the back foot. Figures involving a check taken outside the partner followed by a chassé or side step are very common in Latin-American dances since the partners stand further apart and may indeed both check forward at the same time as in the New York.

111

Shoulder to Shoulder

In this figure as the man checks forward, the lady steps backward (Rumba One (1971), Waikiki Cha Cha Cha (1993)).

Shoulder to Shoulder (man's steps; lady's steps are opposite)			Beat Value	
	Cha Cha Cha	Rumba	CCC	Rumba
Check	1. RF fwd OP (R side)	1. RF fwd OP (R side)	1	1
	2. Replace wt to LF	2. Replace wt to LF turning ¼ to R	1	1
Chassé RLR	3. RF to side ⎤ ¼	3. RF to side	½	2
	4. LF ½ closed ⎥ turn to RF ⎥ to		½	
	5. RF to side ⎦ R		1	
Check				
	6. LF fwd OP (L side)	4. LF fwd OP (L side)	1	1
	7. Replace wt to RF	5. Replace wt to RF turning ¼ to L	1	1
Chassé LRL	8. LF to side ⎤ ¼		½	
	9. RF ½ closed ⎥ turn to LF ⎥ to	6. LF to side	½	2
	10. LF to side ⎦ L		1	

<u>Cha Cha Cha</u> (man's steps)

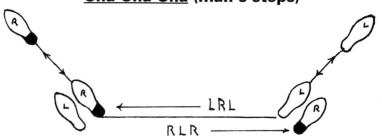

Similar checks outside the partner with a chassé occur in the Mayfair Quickstep (1958); outside checks with a step instead of the chassé are found in the Saunter Together (1975), Westlynn Waltz (1990) and Caribbean Foxtrot (1986).

The New York

The outside check from open promenade position (and counter promenade position) is called the New York (or New Yorker). Both partners check forward at the same time.

New York (man's steps)		Beat Value	
Cha Cha Cha	**Rumba**	**CCC**	**Rumba**
1. RF fwd in ⌉ ⅛ turn to L Open PP⌋	1. As in CCC ⌉ ⅛ turn to L	1	1
2. Replace wt ⌉ ⅜ turn to LF ⌋ to R	2. As in CCC ⌉ ⅜ turn to R	1	1
3-5 Chassé RLR⌋	3. LF to side⌋	½½1	2
6. LF fwd in Open ⌉ ⅛ turn CPP ⌋ to R	4. As in CCC ⌉ ⅛ turn to R	1	1
7. Replace wt to RF ⌉ ⅜ turn 8-10 Chassé LRL ⌋ to L	5. As in CCC ⌉ ⅜ turn to L 6. RF to side⌋	1 ½½1	1 2
Lady does steps 6-10 as man does steps 1-5 and vice versa	Lady does steps 4-6 as man does steps 1-3 and vice versa		

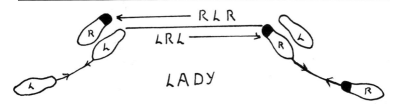

LADY

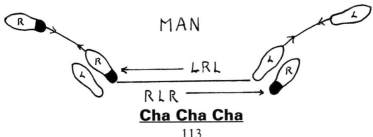

MAN

Cha Cha Cha

There are other forms of the New York. In the Jacqueline Cha Cha Cha (1961) both partners are in shadow position with right and left hands joined. They move across the line of dance performing the same steps - 'on the same leg'. Another variation is the **change of place** - after checking, the partners cross in front and behind moving across the line of dance (Commador Cha Cha Cha (1992)).

The Hand-to-Hand

The hand-to-hand is a backward movement in fallaway position followed by a chassé or side step.

Hand-to-Hand (man's steps; lady's steps are opposite)		Beat Value	
Cha Cha Cha	**Rumba**	**CCC**	**Rumba**

1. RF bk in open ⌉ ¼ turn
    fallaway ⌋ to R
	1. As Cha Cha ⌉ ¼ turn
	    Cha ⌋ to R
		1	1

2. Replace wt to LF ⌉ ¼ turn
3-5 Chassé RLR ⌋ to L
    etc.
	2. As Cha Cha Cha ⌉¼ turn
	3. RF to side ⌋ to R
	    etc.
		1
		½½1
			1
			
			2

(Corrida Cha Cha Cha (1990), Rumba Charlene (1990))

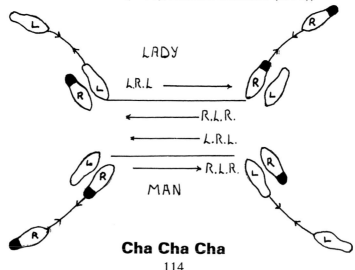

Cha Cha Cha

114

CHAPTER 12

THE VARIOUS DANCES

Section	Dance	Time signature	Tempo (bpm)	
Modern	Waltz	3/4	31	(29-31)
	Slow Foxtrot	4/4	30	(28-31)
	Quickstep	4/4	50	(45-50)
	Tango	2/4	33	(30-34)
	(Viennese Waltz)	3/4	60	(56-64)
(Feet at an angle) Old-Time ------- (Feet parallel)	Old-Time Waltz	3/4	42	(40-44)
	Gavotte	4/4	24	(23-25)
	Two Step	6/8	48	(44-56)
	Mazurka	3/4	42	(42-46)
	Glide	4/4	24	(23-25)
	Saunter	4/4	28	(27-29)
	Blues	4/4	30	(29-31)
	Swing	4/4	48	(45-50)
	Old-Time Tango	2/4	32	(30-33)
Latin-American	Rumba	4/4 or 2/4	28	(26-32)
	Cha Cha Cha	4/4 or 2/4	30	(31-33)
	Samba	2/4 or 4/4	50	(48-54)
	Jive	4/4	44	(35-46)
	Paso Doble	2/4 or 6/8	62	(58-62)

Playing Times

A **track** of 6 sequences of 16 bars plus a 4 bar introduction gives 100 bars of music.

For a quickstep at 50 bpm, playing time is 100/50 = 2 mins.

For a gavotte at 25 bpm, playing time is 100/25 = 4 mins.

Playing Speeds (Tempi)

For examination purposes each sequence dance has a fixed tempo, e.g.:

Quando, Eivona and Universal Quicksteps	50 bpm
Rosslyn, Benita and Glenroy Foxtrots	30 bpm
Tango Magenta	32 bpm
Tango Victoria	33 bpm
Fylde Waltz	40 bpm
Regis Waltz	42 bpm
Lilac Waltz	44 bpm

In ordinary sequence dancing the dances are performed over a range of tempi (see previous table). Slower playing speeds are used for learning purposes, groups of less agile dancers and to suit particular sequence dances. Bill Botham considered that it was unrealistic to aim for a fixed tempo that would cover all sequence quicksteps, tangos or any other style of dance. In general he felt that playing speeds needed to be slower for sequence dancers than for ballroom dancers since having to remember and keep to the sequence required a measure of thinking time.

It is not always easy to judge the speed at which a dance is being played - you need a stopwatch to be sure! The different rhythms and accents often affect the apparent speed. One experienced band leader used to ask his clients if they wanted him to play too fast or two slow! Differences between rhythms are often very subtle - why does one tune get the feet tapping and another seem rather dull? A particular record can be used at the same tempo for a sequence quickstep, swing or jive yet it will suit one better than the others. Even the most articulate musicians find difficulty in expressing these matters accurately in words.

Beats and Bars

In music for dancing there is a regular recurrence of strong and weak **beats** which divide the music into **bars**. Each bar is a rhythmic unit of the same length starting with a strong beat.

116

Duple time has 2 beats, **triple time** 3 beats and **quadruple time** 4 beats per bar. If each beat has the value of a note such as a quaver or a crotchet and can thus be divided into two parts, this is **simple** time. If the beat is 1½, divisible into three parts, this is **compound** time.

The beats and bars are specified by the **time signature**. Waltz time is simple time and the 3/4 symbol indicates that each bar has three beats each of a quarter note (crotchet) in length. Hence the length of the bar is 3 x ¼ notes.

There are four common measures used for dancing:-

(a) Tango and March Time 2/4

Simple duple time - 2 beats of a quarter note each per bar. Counted as 1,2; 1,2; etc. If counted in beats and bars this becomes 1,2; 2,2; 3,2; etc.

Dances in 2/4 time - Tango, Paso Doble, Samba, Habanera, One Step, Polka, Galop, some Rumbas and Cha Cha Chas.

(b) Waltz Time 3/4

Simple triple time - 3 beats per bar, each beat being a ¼ note. Counted as 1,2,3; 2,2,3; 3,2,3; etc.

Dances in triple time - Old-Time, Modern and Viennese Waltzes, Mazurka, Minuet, Fandango.

(c) Common Time 4/4

Simple quadruple time - 4 beats per bar, each beat being a ¼ note. Counted as 1,2,3,4; 2,2,3,4; etc. Counting is sometimes in slows (S) and quicks (Q). (S = 2 beats; Q = 1 beat. Hence for one bar possible timings are SS, SQQ, QQS, QQQQ.)

Dances in common time - Slow Foxtrot, Quickstep, Rumba, Cha Cha Cha, Saunter, Swing, Blues, Charleston, Gavotte, Schottische, Jive, Rock 'n' Roll.

(d) Compound Time 6/8

This is compound duple time (there are other forms of compound time). There are 2 beats to the bar each beat being of 3 x ⅛ notes (1½ crochets or 3 quavers). It is counted as 1,2; 2,2; 3,2; etc. (Less frequently, as 1,2,3,4,5,6; 2,2,3,4,5,6; etc.)

Dances in "compound time" - Two Steps, Marches, Irish Reels, some One Steps, Paso Dobles.

Relations between Modern and Old-Time Dances

The old-time waltz, two step, gavotte and similar dances are performed with the feet at an angle - these are dealt with in the following chapter.

Old-time dances such as saunters, swings and blues are danced with the feet in parallel position. Although they are very popular today, they are largely neglected in dancing manuals. They can be seen as complementing and extending the role of the modern dances. A modern dance such as the **foxtrot** has a clearly defined technique and standard dancing figures - ballroom hold is used and body contact maintained at all times. **Saunters** are played at roughly the same tempo (usually slightly slower) but use various holds and sometimes no hold at all as in solo turns; older figures such as the step and point, twinkle and rotary turn are found in sequences. Some early foxtrots are saunters in all but name. Thus the Pins and Needles Foxtrot is started in Maxina hold; the On Leave Foxtrot (1917) has twinkles, a rotary turn and a release of hold.

1. Waltzes (29-64 bpm)

Modern waltzes are played at 29-31 bpm. More recent dances use ballroom hold and technique and feet are parallel, not at an angle. Older modern waltzes often display what might be called old-time characteristics - movements not involving ballroom hold like solo turns and figures such as the square, step and point and rotary turn.

118

Old-time waltzes are played at a faster tempo of 40-44 bpm and have dancing figures such as the pas de valse, pas glissade and rotary turns. Most of the figures are danced with the feet at an angle to one another. Such waltzes still win prizes at inventive competitions in modern sequence - Magnolia Waltz (1987), Galaxy Waltz (1990).

The **Viennese Waltz** (quick waltz) is played at 56-64 bpm. It uses standard ballroom technique, has standard dancing figures and is classed as a modern dance. (It has not, however, so far been used in sequence dancing - the Viennese Sequence Waltz is really an old-time waltz with some Viennese elements.)

2. Tangos (30-34 bpm)

The tango has South American origins. It contains elements of the habanera (a slow Cuban dance from Havana) and the bolero (a Spanish dance in triple time). It started to become popular as a ballroom dance in the UK about 1912.

Differences between old-time and modern tangos are less marked than the differences between the waltzes. Although they are allocated to different sections by the British Council of Ballroom Dancing they are often danced to the same tango music although "brighter" music tends to be used for the modern tangos. Dance leaders do not always announce whether a particular tango is old-time or modern and many sequence dancers perform them in exactly the same style.

Old-time tangos use figures such as squares and solo turns - body contact is not always maintained. In the Eugene Tango (1950) the man and lady stand almost side by side in a sort of shadow position doing the same steps on the same foot throughout.

Modern tangos use standard ballroom technique: there is a special tango hold and standard figures for the dance. The dancers take longer steps and move in more staccato fashion - there are exaggerated quick turning movements of the head and other parts of the body (see p. 37). The partners stand at an angle to the direction of movement. The man's left foot moves forward in CBMP closing the upper legs together, the following right foot movement is an opening-out movement with the right shoulder leading. The couple move in a gentle curve down the line of dance (see Chapter 3, p. 49).

3. Quicksteps and Swings (45-50 bpm)

The **quickstep** is a happy, carefree sort of dance which has its roots in the one step (1914) and the charleston (1925); it is a foxtrot adapted to a faster tempo. It is played to lively martial music having 4 beats to the bar.

Sequence **swings** are played at roughly the same tempo as the quickstep but with brighter, 'bouncy' music. Many swings have a figure in which the foot is moved to a low aerial position by swinging the leg (called a flick in some scripts). 'Swing' is a term used by jazz musicians to mean an improvisation of melodic rhythm. Dancers will sometimes refer to a couple 'swinging' a quickstep when they make subtle alterations in the timing of the steps. Swing tunes have a firm, rhythmic background with the melody just ahead to give an urgent offbeat. Benny Goodman was called the 'king of swing' in the 1930's - the big bands of the 1930-1945 era played swing music. The American or Lindy Swing is called the Jive or Jitterbug in Britain. The Jive is often danced to quickstep music.

4. Foxtrots, Saunters and Blues (27-31 bpm)

Foxtrots and saunters have a common origin. The name 'saunter' was given to the smooth flowing form of the foxtrot by the 'Dancing Times' about 1916. Early sequence foxtrots and saunters have many common characteristics. The reason for the name 'foxtrot' is not altogether clear; some maintain that the step and heel movements resemble those of a fox, others say the dance takes its name from the stage routines of Harry Fox (1912). Foxtrots and saunters are danced to music in common time with the accent on the first and third beats.

The modern **slow foxtrot** is the most typical of the dances in the 'English style'. It has long gliding casual steps and requires considerable space in the ballroom - it is a dance for good dancers. The beats in the music are not stressed very strongly and the dancer must listen carefully to time his steps correctly. Modern sequence foxtrots took a long time to appear: the first Official Board Handbook of Modern Sequence Dances (1966) did not contain a real modern sequence foxtrot (see Chapter 15).

The **saunter** is a slow graceful dance played at a slower tempo than the foxtrot - it requires good balance. Early saunters are the Yearning Saunter (1919) and the London Moonlight Saunter (1920).

The **blues** has long been known as a ballroom dance. Alex Moore (dancing with his sister) won the Blues Competition at Princes Galleries in London in 1923. The blues is usually played to music in the foxtrot tempo range with more stress on the four beats. The walk has a lilting movement obtained by relaxing the supporting knee followed by a slight rise on the ball of the foot. Some dancing teachers recommend that the forward steps should be taken with slight CBMP.

Some early sequence blues were played in quickstep tempo - Georgella Blues (1951; 44-46 bpm), Manhattan Blues 46-48 bpm). Other early blues are the Lingering Blues (1929; 32-34 bpm), Yale Blues (1927; 34 bpm), Breakaway Blues (1946; 32 bpm).

Classic blues music (late 1880's) has 3 sections of 4 bars each and has certain notes flattened (blue notes). There are breaks for an instrumental flourish or for the singer to say "Oh Lordy" or "Yeah Man" which would be off-putting to the sequence dancer. Commercial blues became all the rage with the appearance of the Memphis Blues and St. Louis Blues in 1909. Tunes for modern sequence blues contain elements of these traditions - they tend to be sentimental songs with a well-marked beat played at a foxtrot tempo.

The slow social rhythm dance described in ballroom dancing manuals is a form of blues without rise or fall. Rhythm and blues (R and B) music is written primarily for dancing - it is often called rock 'n' roll (1950's onward).

With the great revival of old-time dancing after the second world war, several other dances in the foxtrot/ saunter group were arranged:-

Strolls start in a side-by-side position and have many steps danced 'on the same foot'. Examples are the Festival Stroll (1953; 32 bpm), Sunshine Stroll (1966; 24 bpm). The Skater's Stroll (1985; 32-34 bpm) is a line party dance.

(Parades are similar to strolls but played at a faster tempo, e.g. Holiday Parade (1970; 48 bpm).)

Sways are dances with sway figures:- Islington Sway (1950; 32 bpm), Franciscan Sway (1963; 28 bpm), Twyford Sway (1975; 30 bpm).

Glides often start with both partners side-by-side, facing down the line of dance. The Gainsborough Glide (1950; 24-28 bpm) is an official old-time dance and is performed with feet at an angle. The Jubilee Glide (1972; 32 bpm) has a mixture of old-time and modern styles.

There are also twinkles, bumps, jinks, rags, strutters and numerous party dances but these are of minor importance.

5. Paso Dobles, One Steps and Two Steps (44-62 bpm)

The **paso doble** is often called the Spanish one step (although the name means 'double step' in Spanish). It is danced to brisk marching music in 2/4 or 6/8 time (or occasionally 3/4 time) at 58-62 bpm. It is classed as a Latin-American dance despite its relationship to the old-time one steps and two steps. The arms are held somewhat higher than in the normal waltz hold and the lady has less of a backward poise. It is a proud haughty dance and the man should be impassive and upright in demeanour with legs braced more than usual. The man represents the matador, the lady is his cape and the bull is imaginary. Thus the huit is a figure of 8 steps representing the waving of the cape from side-to-side; the appel is a sort of foot stamp without raising the foot from the ground designed to attract the bull's attention.

Paso dobles in sequence form are not too common. The Paso Madrid (1964) and Paso Deena (1974) are official sequence dances; the Pepi Paso (1986) is a recent prize winner.

One steps and two steps are old-time quick marching dances. The distinctions between the two dances are not altogether clear. Some say that one steps are in 2/4 time, two steps in 6/8 time, but this is not always adhered to. Victor Sylvester states that marches (two steps, Gay Gordons, etc.) are danced to rousing military marches whereas one steps are danced to tunes written for ballroom use. Both types of dances are performed in a mixture of the two styles - the feet are in parallel for the marching steps but inclined at an angle for figures like the pas de basque.

The **one step** is a fast marching dance played at about 50 bpm. It was made popular in the USA by Vernon Castle during the first world war. The Castle Walk is a type of one step. The one step was displaced by the quick foxtrot (quickstep) about 1925. There are relatively few sequence one steps - the best known is the Dinky One Step (56 bpm) which is a party dance performed with feet in parallel position. The Harlequin One Step (1958) is a dance with old-time figures; recommended music is the 'Angus Reel' at 50 bpm.

Two steps are more important to the modern sequence dancer since they still appear at regular intervals:- Hampton Two Step (1985; 50 bpm), Solara Two Step (1991; 48 bpm). Two steps almost always include the pas de basque figure and are dealt with in Chapter 13.

There are relatively few **three steps**, the most common being the Eva Three Step (1904; 32 bpm) which consists largely of three walking steps followed by a point in various directions (originally designed for gavotte music at 24 bpm). The most common **four step** is the Marine Four Step which is danced to rousing military marching music played at 56 bpm. Why the dances are called four steps is not altogether clear.

Latin-American Dances

Latin-America comprises those parts of South and Central America, Mexico and the Caribbean Islands which have Spanish or Portuguese as their official language. The Latin-American dances from these areas have a strong, compulsive rhythm and are readily adapted to sequence form.

1. Mambo, Rumba and Cha Cha Cha

Mambo is a ballroom dance derived from the Cuban rumba. It was danced in Cuban ballrooms in the mid-1940's and became popular in Western Europe after 1955. It is a fast tempo ballroom rumba (50-60 bpm) which has not so far been used in sequences. The ballroom rumba is sometimes called the single-beat mambo and the cha cha cha the triple-beat mambo; both these dances are played at a much slower tempo and give rise to many popular modern sequence dances.

The **rumba** (or rhumba) is a very old dance with African and Cuban origins. There are two main ballroom forms - the American or square rumba (1931) and the Cuban rumba (1948); the latter is the version used by modern ballroom and sequence dancers. The rumba became popular in the United States and Britain in the 1930's. It is danced with a smooth supple hip movement with small heavy walking steps. Sequence rumbas are played at 26-32 bpm. The Rumba Royale (1963) is a very early sequence rumba.

The **cha cha cha**, sometimes called the Cuban mambo, is a type of rumba with an extra beat. Its name derives from the basic rhythm of step, step, chassé - often expressed as 'step, step, cha cha cha'. It appeared in America in the 1950's and

124

in Britain in the early 1960's. It is a staccato lively dance giving much room for personal expression. Early sequence forms are the Jacqueline Cha Cha Cha (1961) and the Margarite Cha Cha Cha (1962).

2. Samba, Bossa Nova and Merengue

The **samba** was an instant success when introduced into the USA in 1929; it can be seen as an up-dated version of the strenuous Brazilian Maxixe (1912-1914). It is a gay light-hearted dance in 2/4 time (sometimes 4/4) played at 48-54 bpm. A characteristic feature of the dance is the up and down motion produced by a springy knee action called the 'samba bounce' or 'samba pulse'. The samba walk is a peculiar flat-footed movement in which the dancer moves forward and then pulls back with a body sway, making forward progress rather slow. Popular figures in the sequence sambas are bota fogos, samba whisks and the travelling and circular voltas. Popular sequence sambas are the Samba Miranda (1961) and the Samba Marina (1990).

The **bossa nova** (new beat) is of Brazilian origin (1958-1959); it was a vehicle of social protest in the 1960's. The dance has elements of the samba and the rumba and is performed in 4/4 time at 34-40 bpm. It is danced with a twisting body action (not side-to-side as in the rumba) and without rise or fall. Recent sequence forms are the Bossa Nova Blues (1982), Bossa Nova '87 (1987) and the Bella Bossa Nova (1992). The last two dances include clockwise chassé squares.

The **merengue** is a Caribbean dance performed to music in 4/4 time with accents on the first and third beats. It is a staccato dance with similar motions to the rumba. Its main distinguishing feature is the walk which has the appearance of a limp. The man steps on his left foot, flexing the knee and leaning the body in the same direction. This 'merengue action' is used in several modern sequence dances, e.g. Orpheo Cha Cha Cha (1988), Let's Jive (1993), Katie Cha Cha Cha (1993).

3. The Jive

'Jive' is a general term covering several related dances played to various rhythms in the range 20-60 bpm. As the jitterbug, it was brought to the UK by American and Canadian servicemen in the early 1940's. This was a vigorous dance in which the couples did not move round the floor, and caused complaints from quickstep dancers trying to circulate in the usual way.

The modern ballroom jive is a much more sophisticated dance with its own figures and technique. It is danced in 4/4 time at 35-46 bpm with a tempo of 44 bpm for the standard jives used for examination purposes. It is a North-American rather than a Latin-American dance but it resembles the rumba and cha cha cha in some respects and is conveniently placed in the same class. Like the rumba the lady seems to do all the work while the man does basic steps; the man leads the lady into many of the figures by using his arm - underarm turns, changes of place, stop and go, etc. There are also solo turns for the lady such as the American spin.

It resembles the cha cha cha in being a triple beat dance involving a regular use of chassés although the rhythms used are more complex. One basic one-bar rhythm is:-

	Step	Step	Jive	Chassé
Timing	Q	Q	Q	a	Q
Beat value	1	1	$\frac{3}{4}$	$\frac{1}{4}$	1

This is often extended to $1\frac{1}{2}$ bars by adding an extra chassé. The jive chassé is rather more jerky than the cha cha cha chassé which has a beat value of $\frac{1}{2},\frac{1}{2},1$, counted as Q and Q. In both types of chassé the feet are only half closed on the second step, unlike waltz and quickstep chassés. The jive is danced with the weight well forward, with steps being taken on the ball of the foot with the heel touching or just clear of the floor.

The Jim Jam Jive (1962) is an early novelty jive based on chassés; the Jupiter Jive (1973) is an examination dance.

Jives adapt well to changes in tempo and are often played at slower speeds to suit the more elderly dancers.

CHAPTER 13

THE TRADITIONAL OLD-TIME DANCES

Early dances such as the old-time waltz, gavotte, two step, mazurka, schottishe and polka are danced with the feet at an angle. Three of these dances continue to win awards:-

1. The Gavotte - 4/4 time, tempo 23 - 25 bpm

The gavotte is the slowest of the sequence dances; it is a stately cheerful dance which was popular in the courts of Louis XIV (1638 - 1715)) and Louis XV (1710-1774) where it often followed the minuet. Its basic step is the **pas de gavotte** in which the foot is raised to ankle height on the fourth step (see later). Three new sequence gavottes won awards in 1990.

2. The Two Step - 6/8 time, tempo 44-56 bpm

A dance of American origin, played to rousing military music. The first two step was called the Washington Post (1890's) danced to J. P. Sousa's march of the same name. There were many military two steps from 1900 to 1917 when the dance was gradually replaced by the one step. Many more two steps appeared after the old-time revival in 1945-1950 but from 1965 onwards the modern foxtrot and quickstep became more popular. The essential figure in the two step is the **pas de basque**; many two steps finish with bars of waltzing. Since 1975, 8 two steps have won awards; the latest being the Grenadier Two Step (1993).

3. The Old-Time Waltz - 3/4 time, tempo 40-44 bpm

The old-time waltz is danced at a slower tempo than the Viennese Waltz but faster than the modern waltz. Common figures are the pas de valse, pas glissé and pas glissade and there are aerial figures and zephyr steps. Some championship dances are the Lilac Waltz (1951), Imperial Waltz   Waltz Camay (1958), Regis Waltz (1964) and Northern Star Waltz (1965).

Old-Time Technique

A competent modern sequence dancer needs some knowledge of the five foot positions and the old-time steps and associated technique to perform such dances as may appear. Some points to look out for are:-

(a) Many old-time dances start in **open hold** with partners side-by-side at some distance from one another facing the same way. The man's right hand holds the lady's left hand. The man holds his left hand lightly on his left hip; the lady holds up her gown lightly between right thumb and first finger. Sometimes the dancers are closer together in shadow hold, sometimes they are in normal ballroom hold. The hand holds and positions usually change throughout the dance.

(b) The feet are turned out at 90° to one another and 45° to the body. (This is a modified form of the 180° turnout used in classical ballet since 1820 which requires special exercises to allow the thigh bone to rotate fully in its socket.)

(c) Expert old-time dancers will waltz round in the old style with feet at an angle - the feet step round rather than being swung round by the legs as in the modern waltz. This gives a neat appearance but requires much practice to perform correctly.

(d) Many of the figures involve step closes:-

Pas glissé and balancé	-	step; close without weight
Pas glissade	-	step; close with weight
Pas de valse (waltz step)	-	step; step; close
Pas de gavotte (gavotte step)	-	step; close; step; aerial

(e) In steps such as the forward pas de valse the ball of the foot skims the floor - the heel is then lowered to place the foot flat on the floor.

The Five Positions of the Feet

The Closed Positions

1st Position
(a starting position)

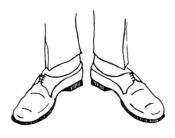

3rd Position

5th Position

The Open Positions

2nd Position
Either foot placed exactly to the side, e.g. LF to side.

4th Position
One foot placed straight forward gives 4th position front; straight backward gives 4th position rear, e.g. LF fwd or RF bk. All the positions may have one or both feet with the toe, ball of foot or heel on the ground.

Intermediate positions are sometimes found, e.g. LF diag fwd.

Aerial positions have one foot off the ground; low, medium and high positions have the foot level with the ankle, calf and knee respectively.

129

Front and Rear Closed Positions

Examples starting from second position

   2nd position

(a) Third position (from2nd position)

RF has moved to
3rd position front
(**Heel** of RF finishes
against instep of LF)

RF has moved to
3rd position rear
(**Instep** of RF finishes
against heel of LF)

(b) Fifth position (from2nd position)

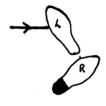 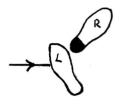

LF has moved to
5th position front
(**Heel** of LF near
big toe of RF)

LF has moved to
5th position rear
(Big **toe** of LF near
heel of RF)

Various Old-Time Figures

(a) Pas glissade (gliding step)

Step; close to 3rd position **with weight**. Often taken to the side.

(b) Pas glissé (another gliding step)

Step; close to 3rd position **without weight**. The closing foot is now free to move in some other direction.

The Magnolia Waltz (1987) has side and forward pas glissés, it finishes with a pas glissade.

(c) Balancé

Step; close to 3rd position **without weight**. This differs from the pas glissé in having a rocking, swaying action - a rise to the ball of the foot on the first step is followed by a lowering at the end of the second step. The Marie Mazurka (1906) and Valse Martine (1951) start with a forward and a backward balancé. The Starlight Gavotte (1993) has a forward balancé with a right foot lead.

(d) Pas de Valse

Step; step; close to 3rd position **with weight**. This is the forward closed change of Chapter 2 in a different guise - it is a straight line figure (rather than triangular) and finishes with the feet at an angle. In the same way it is used to change from a natural to a reverse turn and vice versa.

If the partners are in ballroom hold the lady will do a backward pas de valse while the man does the forward figure. If in side-by-side position (open or shadow holds), they will do the same pas de valse with opposite feet. In Rinking (1939), which is a type of skating dance, the partners take the pas de valse on the same foot moving round in a circle with hands crossed.

(e) Pas de Gavotte

Step; close to 3rd position **with weight**: step; point to low aerial position forward (ankle height with the toe pointing down). The steps should be performed with a gliding action without stiffness or undue haste - the gavotte is a slow graceful dance. The pas de gavotte may be taken with either foot and sometimes involves a turn of $\frac{1}{8}$. The Gavotina (1920's) has both forward and backward pas de gavottes. Recent award-winners are the Lladro Gavotte (1992) and Starlight Gavotte (1993). The championship dance is the Wedgewood Blue Gavotte (1959).

(f) Pas de Zephyr

A step in which the dancer stands on one leg and moves the other with a sweeping action from a backward to a forward position with the foot passing close to the supporting foot (and vice versa). The Lilac Waltz (1951) and Galaxy Waltz (1990) start with a LF fwd step followed by a forward zephyr. The Gainsborough Glide (1950) has both right foot and left foot zephyr steps. The Eugene Tango (1950) has a zephyr turn.

(g) Pas de Basque ('pah de bar' or 'pah der bahsk')

This is a very graceful step found in two steps, schottisches, gavottes, glides and Scottish reels. It is not easy to describe accurately and it is said that no two dancers execute it in quite the same fashion.

Like all springing steps, the knee of the opposite leg must be slightly flexed in preparation. The following three steps are for a left foot pas de basque taken **outward** from the partner:-

1. spring to the side with the LF (with a slight rondé movement);

2. close to RF to LF in 5th position front releasing the LF slightly from the floor;

3. replace the weight to the LF with the toe of the RF pointing downwards.

These three steps would be counted "1 a 2" ($\frac{3}{4}$,$\frac{1}{4}$,1) or "1 and 2" ($\frac{1}{2}$,$\frac{1}{2}$,1) in some scripts.

All steps with a springing hopping or jumping action can be made easier (and less attractive) by replacing the spring with a step. A simplified version for the novice sequence dancer is:-

1. LF to side in a semi-circular manner (rondé).

2. Swing RF across in front of the LF with the toe pointing downwards.

The Bilmay Two Step (1950's) has this modified figure. Early scripts of the Boston Two Step (1908) have "Jetté outwards and inwards 2 bars" but later versions have "pas de basque outwards and inwards". The Grenadier Two Step (1993) starts with the same two figures with a forward close in between.

The pas de basque is found in the Butterfly Gavotte (1950), the Gainsborough Glide (1950) and the Latchford Schottische (1909).

Old-Time Waltz Turns

Many old-time dances such as the Barn Dance, Veleta (1900), Military Two Step (1906), Gay Gordons (1907) and Savoy Schottische (1950) finish with a finale of several bars of waltzing. Natural turns are used which give a complete turn over 6 steps.

The old-time waltz turn, with the feet at an angle, consists of:-

(a) a **rotary** half turn in which the man is moving backward. He is on the inside of the turn and travels less;

(b) a **progressive** half turn in which he is moving forward on the outside of the turn and travels further down the ballroom.

The lady dances the progressive half turn while the man performs the rotary half turn and vice versa.

Natural Rotary Half Turn (Man's steps)	Turn	Timing
1. LF to side, sltly bk, turning R	⅛ R	S
2. RF closes to LF in 5th position rear	⅛ R	S
3. Rising on the toes with weight on the LF, pivot to the right finishing with the RF in 5th position front	¼ R	S

Natural Progressive Half Turn (Man's steps)	Turn	Timing
1. RF fwd between partner's feet, turning R	⅛ R	S
2. LF to side still turning R	⅛ R	S
3. RF closes to LF in 5th position front	¼ R	S

The reverse turns have similar steps on the opposite foot with a turn to the left. Dancers change from a natural to a reverse turn in ballroom waltzing by using the appropriate pas de valse.

In sequence waltzes the partners sometimes perform solo turns independently of one another, e.g. Lilac Waltz (1951). An **inward** solo turn is **towards** the partner whereas an **outward** solo turn is **away** from the partner. With figures taken solo or in loose hold there is often more progression than when dancing in ballroom hold.

134

Waltz Finales

In the final bars of waltzing in the various sequence dances, some dancers use the natural rotary turn with parallel feet positions (Exercise 6, Chapter 2, p. 30) as an alternative to the turns in the previous section. Other dancers cross the feet instead of closing to parallel position to assist the turns.

If the dance has started in open position with partners side-by-side, this position needs to be regained after the waltz turns. This is achieved by the man dancing $1\frac{1}{2}$ natural turns (3 bars) with a pas de valse (1 bar) while the lady does two complete turns (4 bars).

Normal waltzing is carried out in 3/4 time - there are 3 beats in the bar and a step to each beat giving a count of 1,2,3; 2,2,3; etc. A complete waltz turn of 6 steps will occupy 2 bars.

When waltzing in other times, the waltz timing has to be modified as follows:-

(a) Tango and March Time 2/4 (some Two Steps)

Count	1	a	2	,	2	a	3
Beat Value	$\frac{3}{4}$	$\frac{1}{4}$	1		$\frac{3}{4}$	$\frac{1}{4}$	1

2 bars are needed to complete the 6 steps of the waltz turn.

(b) Common Time 4/4 (Latchford Schottische (1909))

Count	1	a	2	,	3	a	4	,	2	a	2	,	3	a	4
Beat Value	$\frac{3}{4}$	$\frac{1}{4}$	1		$\frac{3}{4}$	$\frac{1}{4}$	1		$\frac{3}{4}$	$\frac{1}{4}$	1		$\frac{3}{4}$	$\frac{1}{4}$	1

The waltz turn is completed in 1 bar (2 turns above).

(c) Compound Time 6/8 (Gay Gordons (1907))

Count	1	a	2	2	a	3
Beat Value	$\frac{3}{4}$	$\frac{1}{4}$	1	$\frac{3}{4}$	$\frac{1}{4}$	1

2 bars are needed for the complete waltz turn.

Salutations

In old-time and square dancing the partners **acknowledge** one another by the man bowing and the lady curtseying. This is performed during the 4-bar (or other length) introduction and sometimes forms an integral part of the dance, e.g. Latchford Schottische (1909) and Valse Martine (1951). At the end of the dance the lady turns under the man's left arm before the salutations. In modern sequence dancing the bow and curtsey are rarely used although some dancing teachers acknowledge their partners in the 4-bar introduction before the sequence proper.

The Bow

The man turns to face the lady with his feet in 1st position. He then slowly inclines the upper part of his body with his arms hanging loosely at his side; he then returns slowly to the erect position without any appearance of stiffness.

A more elaborate bow is achieved by moving the left foot to the side and closing the right foot to 3rd position front, at the same time drawing the right arm across the body at waist level inclining the body from the hips. The bow is completed by slowly straightening the body and stepping forward with the RF closing the LF to 3rd position rear. In old-time tangos and saunters a parallel foot position is used.

The Curtsey

The lady faces her partner and moves her left foot behind her right foot with the heel slightly off the floor. She then relaxes and straightens her knees looking towards her partner all the time.

In the **deep curtsey** she glides her right foot to the side and moves the left foot to the rear with a slight circular action (rondé) without weight. She then bends the right knee, lightly holding her dress in front. She now transfers her weight to the left leg, rising slowly with a curved inclination of the head, releasing the dress. She then closes her right foot to left foot in 3rd position front.

136

The Mazurka

This Polish dance in triple time was introduced into European ballrooms in the 1850's. It is danced with brio and elan with much stamping of feet and clicking of heels. The main step now used in mazurkas is the pas de mazurka which consists of:- step; close; forward aerial step; hop and fouetté - counted 1, 2 and 3. The fouetté is a movement in which the foot is 'whipped' sharply to the front or back of the supporting leg in low aerial position.

LF Pas de Mazurka (Man's steps)	Timing
1. LF fwd	1
2. Close RF to 3rd position rear	$\frac{1}{2}$
3. LF fwd in low aerial position	$\frac{1}{2}$
4. Hop on the RF and bring the LF sharply back to the calf of the R leg with the toe pointing down	1

The Columbine Mazurka (1976; 42 bpm) has both straight and curving LF steps. In the Marie Mazurka (1906; 46 bpm) and Varsoviana (48 bpm) step 4 is often modified by pointing the LF above the right instep instead of whipping it behind the right calf. The mazurka step is not easy to execute correctly and there are relatively few sequence mazurkas.

The Polka

The polka is a Czech dance in 2/4 time, popular in Bohemia in the 1830's; some 10 years later it was all the rage in London and Paris but it fell from favour after 1910. The polka turning figure involves three steps on the first three half beats with a hop on the fourth. It is still danced in the square dance called the Carnival (1895) which contains a section based on the Berlin Polka (1894). It now appears in a much modified form in party dances such as Fiona's Polka (1966) and the Pit-Pat Polka (1983). The Santa Fe Quickstep (1988) has a polka-type twinkle. In the quickstep, **polka rhythm** is "and QQ" ($\frac{1}{2},\frac{1}{2},1$) and **polka movement** is the bouncing action usually associated with this rhythm.

The Schottische

The schottische is sometimes known as the German polka. It is played in 2/4 time at 24-36 bpm - slower than the polka. It is a sort of hopping waltz. The Barn Dance was known in America as the Military Schottische and may have been influenced by the Scottish Highland Schottische. Recent sequence dances are the Savoy Schottische (1950) and Empress Schottische (1964).

Old-Time and Modern Sequence Dancing Compared

Old-time sequence dancing is still very popular although much less so than the modern style. Its interests are well served by the 'Society for the Preservation and Appreciation of Old-Time Music and Dancing' (The Old-Time Society) which publishes a newsletter giving news of current events, dance club reports and a dance diary.

Old-time dancing appeals to those who place great store on order, formality, politeness and appreciation of the values of the past. It is at the opposite pole to disco dancing or the gyrations of scantily-clad couples which sometimes passes for modern ballroom dancing. Formal or evening dress is worn (sometimes with gloves) and the partners acknowledge one another (bow and curtsey) before the dance; the national anthem is played. Like modern sequence dancing sessions, few couples sit out and refreshments form a welcome break to the dancing; few people patronise the bar.

The differences between old-time and modern sequence dancing can be seen more clearly by looking at the programmes for the North Star Dancing Club Festival held at Weston-super-Mare in 1991. This was a national event consisting of both old-time and modern sequence dancing sessions in two different ballrooms in one and the same building.

Analysis of Festival Dances

Class	Age range of dances	Festival	
		Old-Time	Modern
Early	1900 - 1949	30	0
Transitional	1950 - 1974	81	16
Late	1975 plus	6	101*
	Total dances	**117**	**117**

BCBD Class	Type of dance		
Old-Time	OT Waltz, OT Tango, Saunter, Blues, Swing, Gavotte, Two Step, Mazurka, Schottische, Glide, Sway, etc.	109	34
Modern	Mod Waltz, Mod Tango, Quickstep, Slow Foxtrot, (Viennese Waltz)	8	56
Latin- American	Rumba, Cha Cha Cha, Samba, Jive (Paso Doble, Bossa Nova)	0	27
	Total dances	**117**	**117**

* 79 from 1989, 1990 or 1991

Eleven dances were common to both programmes: Lilac Waltz, Mayfair Quickstep, Tango Serida, Tango Las Vegas, Melody Foxtrot, Saunter Together, Saunter Reve, Kaybee Saunter, Balmoral Blues, Bambi Blues and Sindy Swing.

The **Old-Time** programme was made up of old-time dances with a few early quicksteps and foxtrots. Most of the dances were arranged before 1975, several from the 1900-1920 era. Dances from 1975 or later were:- Kaybee Saunter, Saunter Adele, Saunter Together, Tango Las Vegas, Sindy Swing, Edwardian Gavotte. In general dances at old-time sessions tend to be selected from a large but more or less fixed repertoire. The introduction of new dances is a slow process and it is not too difficult to resume dancing again after a few months absence.

The **Modern** programme consisted mainly of dances arranged after 1975 with a majority from the last three years. Dances from before 1975 were:- Universal Quickstep, Mayfair Quickstep (twice), Suzanne Quickstep, Melody Foxtrot, Waltz Cathrine, Woodside Waltz, Engagement Waltz (twice), Tango Serida, Sally Ann Cha Cha Cha, Samba Miranda, Saunter Reve, Bambi Blues, Balmoral Blues, Lilac Waltz (OT).

In advanced modern sequence dancing the programmes change fairly rapidly as some 45 new dances are introduced every year. Any prolonged absence from the dances means an extensive catching-up exercise. It is often said that there are too many new dances. On the other hand, attendances rise rapidly when the new dances appear. Would dancers come on fewer nights per week to the dances if the input of new dances was reduced?

Social Sequence Dancing Sessions include mainly dances from the 1950-1975 period with some earlier dances such as the Square Tango or Lingering Blues. Many of the dancers have had no instruction of any kind although many show considerable dancing ability. The programmes tend to be fairly static. In licensed premises there is usually no leader and if the organist moves too far ahead of his clientele no-one will get up to dance. In social clubs the members may only be dancing one night per week and will not welcome too much change.

Old-time and social sequence dancing sessions have more or less settled programmes selected from a fixed repertoire of dances. In contrast the modern sequence dancers can be seen to be moving forward with the times like a comet shedding a trail of once-popular sequence dances.

CHAPTER 14

FINER POINTS OF TECHNIQUE

Technique

Technique may be defined as "the ensemble of the mechanics of dancing". In practical terms to have good technique is to dance according to the theoretical principles laid down by the various dancing associations.

Style

Style is the appearance of the dancers at rest and in motion - it is not quite the same thing as technique. Good style is something innate above and beyond a mastery of basic principles. You can have good technique with only moderate style but you cannot have good style without good technique.

Poise

Poise is the position of the body in relation to the feet - it varies to some extent in the different dances. The lady in modern dancing has to a greater or lesser extent a backward poise produced by arching the spine from just below the shoulder blades.

Balance

Balance is the correct distribution of the weight of the body. It is essential to achieve a smooth transference of weight from one foot to the other in performing the various dancing figures. Couples with good balance look better and dance more easily and safely.

Basic Stance

The **man** should stand upright with the feet close together. The body should be slightly braced at the waist but the shoulders should remain free and not hunched. The head should be in an upright position with the eyes looking over the lady's shoulder.

The lady's stance is similar to that of the man but her head and shoulders lean slightly backwards (backward poise). The head is turned slightly to the left - it should never be turned to the right in the normal dancing position.

Arms

The position of the arms depends to some extent on the height and build of the partners. The man's left arm should be held at slightly more than a right angle to the elbow for the waltz, quickstep and foxtrot; the right arm should be placed below the lady's left shoulder blade. In the tango the man holds the lady more on his right hand side and the hold is more compact. The left arm is angled more sharply and the right hand moves further round the lady's waist. The man's left hand should hold the lady's right hand with the palms together and the wrists straight. They should be held at a point in between the heights of the two faces.

Knees

The knees should be relaxed except when the leg is fully extended in a stride. (Relaxing is a softening movement whereas bending shortens the height.) The legs should appear straight to the onlooker - dancing with bent knees leads to incorrect balance and the dancer seems to be leaning forward. The legs should be swung from the hips to allow proper use of the heel rather than the ball of the foot.

Feet

In modern dancing the feet should be parallel. In moving forward the body should move slightly before the foot - do not move the leg first and then follow with the body. The feet should brush one another in passing.

More Advanced Dancing Technique

Technique is a rather general term referring to the way in which good dancers perform the various dances. The essentials of good technique are codified in the dancing charts for each figure which set out in considerable detail the experience gained by ballroom dancers over the years. Students working towards the examinations of the various dancing associations study and practise the principles laid down in these charts under the guidance of a trained teacher. Some insight into the finer points of dancing, such as footwork, rise and fall and sway, can be gained by studying a dancing chart. This will provide a basis for further study by the aspiring sequence dancer and indicate what should be looked out for in the performance of experts.

Dancing Charts

Rewriting the table of 123 chassé turn of page 35 we have:-

Man	123 Chassé Reverse Turn			
Step	Feet positions	Alignment	Amount of Turn	Rhythm
1	LF fwd	Facing DC	Start to turn L	S
2	RF to side	Backing DW	¼ between 1 & 2	Q
3	LF closes to RF	Backing LOD	⅛ between 2 & 3	Q

Notice that the angle of turn is given both as a fraction ($\frac{3}{8}$ altogether) and also in terms of alignments.

A chart of this figure for the quickstep would give the following extra information:-

Man	123 Chassé Reverse Turn			
Step	Footwork	Rise and Fall	Sway	CBM
1	HT	Rise e/o 1	St	1
2	T	Up on 2	to L	
3	TH	Up on 3	to L	
		Lower e/o 3		

Preceded by:- Natural Turn with Hesitation, Reverse Pivot, Double Reverse Spin.

Followed by:- Progressive Chassé, Reverse Pivot, Quarter Turn to Left.

Notice the use of the following abbreviations:-

H - Heel; T - Toe; HT - Heel, Toe; TH - Toe, Heel; e/o - end of; St - Straight.

Charts for modern waltzes, quicksteps and slow foxtrots use these categories. In charts for tangos and Latin-American dances footwork is set out in a rather different way and headings for rise and fall, sway and CBM are not used -more information is given about holds and movements of arms and body.

Footwork

The first step has footwork HT. Footwork is defined as the part of the foot in contact with the floor at any particular time. Heel, Toe for this step means that the heel meets the ground first and then there is a follow-through on to the toe (and the ball of the foot to facilitate the turn).

Step 2 is taken on the toe and step 3 first on the toe and then the heel is lowered (TH). Notice how footwork is closely related to rise and fall (at one time they used to be treated together). Steps with rise are usually taken first on the toes, steps with lowering finish on the heel.

Footwork is a rather complex subject and needs explanation and demonstration by a teacher. A few generalisations may be made however:-

(a) Slow forward walking steps have footwork H. This assumes that the rest of the foot lowers after the heel as walking proceeds.

(b) Slow forward steps with rise or turn have footwork HT. The toe and ball of foot are employed in the rising or turning process.

(c) Quick forward steps and side steps often involve a rise and are usually TH.

(d) Backward steps are always taken toe first and have footwork T or TH.

144

Footwork THT is found in the man's backward step of a pivot turn. The turn occurs on the ball of the foot with the heel lightly touching the floor.

It is fortunate that reasonable footwork comes naturally to many dancers without study; it does however require supple feet and insteps. Good footwork makes dancing easier to perform, safer and more pleasing to the eye.

Rise and Fall

Rise and fall is an elevation and lowering of the body to give a graceful undulation. It should be felt in the body as a whole not just the feet - it involves feet, knees and some stretching of the trunk.

The chart for the chassé turn shows a rise at the end of step 1 maintained on steps 2 and 3; the body is lowered at the end of step 3. This is a fairly rapid rise since the quickstep is a fast dance with plenty of body swing on the turns.

The rise in the reverse waltz turn (three slow steps) would be higher but more gradual - start to rise at the end of 1; continue to rise on 2 and 3; lower at end of 3 (some quickstep figures have this more gradual rise - in the quarter turn to the right the rise occurs over steps 2, 3 and 4).

Step 1 for the lady is given as RF bk, with rise and fall written as "Rise e/o 1 NFR". NFR stands for **no foot rise** - the rise occurs in the body with the supporting foot kept flat. NFR commonly occurs between steps 1 and 2 in the inside (backward) half of many turns.

Rise and fall is one of the more controversial topics in ballroom dancing. It is difficult to describe in words and strict adherence to the book may produce a jerky unnatural action. Rise and fall should be a smooth natural movement arising from correct body use - it should not appear 'forced'. According to Arthur Milner, "it is just as bad to rise too much as too little".

145

Sway

Sway is achieved by inclining the whole of the body from the feet upwards. It should not be taken from the hips - there should be a feeling of 'body stretch'. Good sway action has a lot to do with balance and control as well as imparting a pleasing look to the dancer's motion. In many turns (not spins) the dancers lean towards the centre of the turn to counteract what is called (incorrectly) the centrifugal force of the turn - thus in the chart the sway is to the **left** on steps 2 and 3 for the **left** (reverse) turn for the man.

Notice that step 1 is taken with CBM as with nearly all turns.

The general rule is to sway for 2 steps:-

(a) to the **right** after a **RF** CBM step;

(b) to the **left** after a **LF** CBM step.

Some figures such as the impetus turn have sway on only one step, others such as spin and pivot turns have no sway at all.

The amount of sway is relatively small being greatest in the waltz. Much larger amounts of sway appear in sway figures used in saunters, swings and many other dances (Kingfisher Saunter (1990), Saga Waltz (1988).

Most of the material in this chapter refers to the waltz, quickstep and slow foxtrot. In the tango there is no rise or fall or body sway and the shoulders should be kept as level as possible. Since there is no rise and fall, 'ball of foot' is used instead of 'toe' in describing footwork in tango scripts.

CHAPTER 15

THE GROWTH OF MODERN SEQUENCE DANCING IN THE MANCHESTER AREA

It has been said that Lancashire is the home of modern sequence dancing, which is true enough I would say, but we can narrow this down to places such as Liverpool and Manchester - Liverpool will have its own story.

The name 'modern sequence' was coined many years before the then Official Board approved of its use in competitions, etc. A lot of dances in the early days (before I joined the Manchester M.C's Club) consisted of a mixture of old time and modern movements, and a more apt name would be 'popular sequence'. But they were danced to modern timing, though the hold would be released in some of them, and it was no wonder that the modern ballroom teachers of the day were not interested in this type of dancing. Nevertheless, it was becoming increasingly popular with the dancing public.

However, let us go back to 1938 where, at Blackpool, the winning dance was called the Hoop-a-La by Alec Hooper. This was a dance in quickstep tempo and it became very popular in the Manchester area and elsewhere. It was altered slightly by the modern dancers introducing a spin movement into the dance.

In 1948 Marjorie Wantling won the ESTD Trophy with the Waltz Calvalcade. Although this was danced to modern waltz tempo it had many old time characteristics in it. As far as I know, round about the same time her father, Arthur Wantling, a noted Manchester teacher, brought out his Magenta Tango - a truly modern sequence dance and also very popular.

If one looked back in 1948 to the dancing advertisements in the Manchester City News, there would be about 40 dances advertised - old time and popular sequence - from which one could pick and choose from the various halls in the district. Amongst them would be one at which the M.C's were Bill and May Botham.

The M.C's at these halls were an assorted lot. Some, like Bill and May, were members of one or the other of the professional teachers' societies. Others were not qualified in this official sense but the mere fact that they had a 'following' gave them some sort of standing.

The old time 'boom' was well in its stride but dances with a modern flavour and timing were gradually increasing in number. Some M.C's stuck rigidly to old time, others to popular sequence, but the majority mixed the two and, in any case, some did not know the difference. There was a certain amount of jealousy amongst some M.C's. If an M.C. visited the 'home' M.C. he would suspect the visiting M.C. of coming to steal his latest new dance - and probably his suspicions were justified! It did not seem to occur to these people that it would be much more pleasant, and to the advantage of all, if M.C's got together for the good of themselves generally. Then, of course, there was the natural animosity of the qualified professional to the M.C's he regarded as 'cheapjacks' who probably had never had a dancing lesson from an expert. Later on, though, there was to be an association of 'unattached' M.C's in the Manchester area.

In the early 50's I heard of such dances as the Waltz Deluxe, Moderna Waltz, Gwenneth Waltz, Midnight Waltz, Tennessee Waltz, Magenta Waltz. A few of them would be by local arrangers in modern waltz tempo but still retaining the old time style in parts - apart from the Magenta Waltz. This was arranged by a well-known southern teacher, who did not put his name to the script but it was supposed to be arranged by Michael Gwynne. This dance became a close rival to the Waltz Marie.

It was in 1952 that I started to take an interest in dancing and attended medals classes to give me an insight into the modern style. When I visited dance halls featuring sequence dancing, some of them still had some old time dances on their programmes but popular sequence was gradually taking over. Bill and May Botham ran a script service, the 'Bilmay Script Service', and it was in 1952 that I wrote to Bill Botham for half a dozen or more scripts of the day having ambitions to be an M.C. one day.

Bill was also advertising the Fellowship of Sequence Dance Instructors (FSDI) inviting M.C's and club leaders to join. I was interested in this and wrote to him asking if I could join. I was accepted as a 'trainee'. Bill issued a booklet each month for members of FSDI. This contained a few scripts, plus articles on dancing of which he was a master. The booklet was called the 'Sequence Dance World'. Bill and May Botham arranged at least two dozen dances and probably their most popular was a party-type dance called the Bilmay Two Step. In the late 40's Bill had a weekly feature in the Manchester City News called 'On with the Dance' which usually included a dance script - mostly old time.

In March 1953 the Manchester M.C's Club was formed holding monthly meetings and in September of that year I was invited to attend, thus starting my long association with the Club. There, in a hall in Paradise Street, Salford, I met the President (Bill Hunter), the Chairman (Terry Drogan) and a founder member (Arthur Jones), also Bill and May Botham. Bill was only a small man, never really fully fit, but his energy was amazing. It was he who thought of the idea of bringing M.C's together for these meetings and he claimed that the Club was the first of its type in the country.

In 1953 Bill brought out a booklet of scripts, the 'M.C's Handbook', containing old time dances and a few popular sequence dances such as the Alistan Waltz and Maryland Foxtrot arranged by Stan Powell of Dudley, the Waltz Marie (original version) by Joe Senior of Stretford, the Tudor Quickstep by Bill Hunter who also arranged the Sapphire Foxtrot, Picador Tango, Gaiety Quickstep, the Bee Bee Quickstep and the Melody Foxtrot (not to be confused with another Melody Foxtrot which came out a few years later and which became popular all over the country). Also in the handbook were the Ricardo Tango, the Georgella Blues arranged by George and Ella Berwick, The Del Rosa Tango arranged by Len Banks and the Winfield Quickstep arranged by Edith Winfield Taylor. The Ricardo Tango was introduced at the Clegg School of Dancing by Len Meadows.

The Waltz Marie, a modern sequence waltz, created quite a big impression on the dancing public. It was introduced by Len

Meadows at the Levenshulme Palais where he was the M.C. Some of the M.C's present took the dance back to their various classes and, inevitably, some discrepancies crept into their versions. Bill Botham was approached to script the dance - the authentic version being published, as mentioned, in the M.C's Handbook. When it reached the South, some of the old time teachers introduced an Allemande in bars 11 and 12 instead of the solo turn for the lady. They resented the fact that modern sequence was ousting old time and it was even played faster than normal. Even in the Manchester area a normal reverse turn was used in bars 11 and 12, thus bringing the dance in line with modern technique.

Other popular dances going the rounds were the Waltz Russelle by Fred Moran and named after the Russell Street Academy, and the Hallmark Foxtrot arranged by Bill Hall of Stretford. Some of the local arrangers were in the then Empire Society. There were also such dances as the Waltz Superbe, Norvic Tango, Noretta Foxtrot, Waltz Norma, Grosvenor Quickstep all arranged by Norman Knowles; the Winter Waltz, Velmere Tango, Adelphi Foxtrot amongst others by Jim Davies; and Mr. Perfect arranged the Beverley Waltz and Wilton Foxtrot.

In 1955 Bill Botham organised an Inventive Dance Competition amongst the FSDI members. They were invited to send their entries to the Head Office and the scripts would be judged by a panel without seeing the arrangers actually dance their entries. The winning dance was the Alkirk Quickstep by Arthur Jones; he took the name from a band of the day - Al Kirkland. The Waltz Charmaine by Terry Drogan was entered but was an also-ran. I'm sure it failed because the script was not clear. When the script was clarified later on the dance spread all over the country and became very popular.

In March 1956 I was appointed Honorary Secretary of the Manchester M.C's Club and have remained so ever since. In the same year the Club held its first Annual Ball which included quite a few old time dances along with the Waltz Cotillon which, amazingly, was included every year until 1963. In 1957 the Ball programme included such dances as the Winfield Quickstep, Denry Quickstep (arranged by Rene Buckley, a local lady), Empire Foxtrot (by Terry Drogan), Tea for Two, Alkirk

Quickstep, Georgella Blues, Magenta Tango, Melody Foxtrot (from Birkenhead), Gaiety Quickstep and Manhattan Blues. It is interesting to note that the Manhattan Blues was originally a 12 bar sequence and was included as such in the 'Scottish M.C's Handbook of Old Time and Sequence Dances' published about 1953. However, as sequence dances were predominantly in 16 bars, someone added 4 bars to the front of it to make it more presentable to the dancing public.

In 1957 the Broadway Quickstep by Edith Farmer was included in many Ball programmes.

In 1958 we saw the Waltz D'Laine arranged by the new Chairman, Walter Schofield. Further dances arranged by him were the Tango Torina, Gaytime Quickstep and Whitfield Foxtrot. Terry Drogan had left the M.C's Club to form another, the National Alliance of Sequence Dancing (NASD), of which he became President. This was Manchester based and regarded as a sister club as many M.C's were members of both clubs.

In 1958 we had such dances as the Patricia Quickstep by George Hague of Stockport, the Priscilla Blues by Joe Collier, and the Golden Tango - all in the Ball programme of that year - plus the Waltz Charmaine, Waltz D'Laine, Empire Foxtrot, etc.

In 1959 the Tango Capri made its appearance on the Ball programme, together with the Carolina Waltz, the Club Quickstep (arranged specially for the M.C's Club). The Iris Foxtrot by Terry Drogan made its first appearance on the programme also in that year. Although the Iris Foxtrot had unusual timing in 4 or 5 bars, it became tremendously popular in many areas.

Two Liverpool M.C's (John and Ida Hill) joined the Manchester Club. They were M.C's at the Tower Ballroom, New Brighton and their contributions to modern sequence included the Arizona Quickstep, Jonida Cha Cha, Tango Seville and Golden Festival Tango. The programmes at the Tower Ballroom were noted for their modern sequence content. One of the Club members arranged the Tower Swing which was then featured at the Tower Ballroom. Alan and Brenda Holt were another couple new to the Club. Their arrangements included El Paso, December Foxtrot, Waltz Suzanne, Waltz Madelaine, Rumba

Continental and the Tango Majorca. Also appearing about that time were the Waltz Cherie, Waltz Annette, Whispering Tango and Blues Foxtrot - all local dances.

In 1960 the Allied Dancing Association was the first official society to form a modern sequence branch and its syllabus included a Manchester dance - the Blues Foxtrot. Other dances in the early 60's were the Granada Quickstep, Autumn Tango, Lilac Tango, the Sunshine Swing, Happy Cha Cha, Homecoming Waltz (Len Banks), the introduction of the Twist brought the Blues Twist and the Party Twist whilst the Madison brought the Club Madison and the Madison Swing - all Manchester dances.

Modern sequence dances were coming out in increasing numbers. Some of the official societies held their competitions on first, second and third prizewinning dances in any style; not as today - in three separate sections, some of them having a leaning towards modern sequence.

Jack and Elsie Richardson joined the Manchester Club in 1962. They were from Huddersfield - Jack being the Secretary of NASD and later becoming the Chairman of the Yorkshire Sequence Dance Federation. They arranged some popular modern sequence dances including the Delia Waltz, Blue Moon Foxtrot, Celebration Waltz, White Rose Waltz, Souvenir Foxtrot and Linden Quickstep, amongst others, and also a few Latin dances.

In 1962 NASD held its first modern sequence competition and the 'Pennine Trophy' was won by the Kingston Quickstep, second prize going to Albert and Ellen Ford with their Waltz Doreen. The Bilmay Script Service and its 'Sequence Dance World' were responsible for the spread of sequence dances, as was the Michael Gwynne Script Service (which, over the years, must have published about 30 Manchester dances) and Holland Brockbank with his Brockbank Lane Service.

Dances with a modern sequence flavour were usually termed 'Manchester Dances' outside the area. When the Kingston Quickstep reached Scotland (amongst other places) I was contacted by Bert Finlay of Kirkcaldy who was the dance instructor of the Glasgow and District M.C's Club. He required an authentic script of the Kingston Quickstep for teaching purposes. Later on I was invited to the home of Mr. and Mrs. Finlay and stayed for 2 weeks. We went dancing in Kirkcaldy, Falkirk and Burntisland where Bert ran a Saturday weekly dance. Some Manchester dances were on the programmes. Eventually we visited the Clarion Club in Glasgow where the Scottish M.C's and Glasgow and District held their meetings but on different days. There I met Mr. and Mrs. Fanning, arrangers of the Woodside Waltz and other dances. I also met the President of the Scottish M.C's Association, Billy Smith. He was 83 years old at the time and was the arranger of the St. Bernard's Waltz. This dance is included in the Scottish M.C's Handbook giving his name as the arranger.

To my mind Bert Finlay was one of the leading figures in the promotion of modern sequence in many parts of Scotland. One Saturday evening in the Colinswell Hall, Burntisland the programme consisted entirely of Manchester dances, all arranged by myself. This was in 1964, nearly 30 years ago. No doubt some of the present day arrangers would be able to do this also.

Further 'Pennine Trophy' winners were the Rose Lane Waltz (1963) arranged by Ann Beardsworth, Saunter Elite (1964) by Fred and Doris Kirkby, the Waltz Elaine (1965) by Dennis and Joan Rothwell, and the Waltz Etelle (1966) by Rodney and Nellie Hargreaves.

In 1965 modern sequence dancing had become so popular that the Official Board could no longer ignore it. In September a committee reported on modern sequence recommendations - one being that a "new classification of dancing, Modern Sequence, be incorporated into the Official Board rules".

Alex Moore, a noted modern teacher, had, from time to time, published some dance movements in a 16 bar sequence which would be of assistance to dance teachers and their classes. A name was sometimes given to these movements and we had the River Tango and the Happy Feet Quickstep by him. In his August 1965 Monthly Letter Service, he published this comment:-

"Of recent years many teachers have taken popular figures of one of the modern dances and arranged them into a 16 bar sequence. Many continental teachers will remember that when a new dance appeared on the scene I usually taught it to them in a 16 bar sequence and some teachers found this was an easier way to learn and to teach a new dance.

Modern sequence dancing has now a very large following in this country and pupils enjoy dancing modern steps and dances in the form of a sequence. One advantage is that it makes it unnecessary for the man to have the skill to lead his partner."

A few months later he wrote:-

"Modern sequence dancing is here to stay, possibly for a very long time. The Official Board is about to standardise a number of these dances so that the same ones are taught throughout the country. My advice to teachers is to give it a try."

I think the Official Board had only a vague idea of what modern sequence might entail and in some quarters it was even suggested that the Old Time Advisory Board should control it - such was the uncertainty at the time. I suppose the reason for this was they were used to old-time sequence dancing.

The Manchester M.C's Club was dancing and supporting modern sequence as quite a few dances originated in the area and, naturally, were being featured by the Club. The Scottish M.C's Association was one of the prime movers in the cry for recognition of modern sequence. They were knocking at the Official Board's door asking for clarification, guidance, and for dances they would be allowed to use for competitions.

In 1965, some months before the Official Board approved of modern sequence, 'Dance News', which hitherto seemed to fight shy of mentioning modern sequence, started printing a few articles on the progress being made by modern sequence and what was happening in relation to the Official Board. Also in that year the DTA carried out a survey to establish what dances could be used for modern sequence competitions, etc. and Walter Whitman of 'Dance News' suggested the Scottish M.C's

154

Association could possibly furnish scripts closer to the mark and also that the Manchester M.C's Club could possibly supply some test dances. The Club Chairman, Walter Schofield, wrote to 'Dance News' saying he would like to see a complete investigation by the Official Board, or any professional society, into modern sequence dancing. He said that, given the right treatment, modern sequence could open up a new era and a means of conserving the English style. It was in 1965 that the Official Board finally recognised and authorised modern sequence.

In February 1966 the Scottish M.C's Association held an Open Amateur Modern Sequence Competition, in accordance with Official Board rules, at the Albert Ballroom Glasgow. This included a 4 dance modern sequence competition; the dances used were the Broadway Quickstep, Woodside Waltz and 2 Manchester dances - the Blues Foxtrot and the Red Rose Tango. (In 1968 another similar competition was held at Singer's Hall, Clydebank. The 4 dance competition this time included the Laura Waltz, Rosita Cha Cha, Universal Quickstep and the Red Rose Tango.)

In 1966 the Official Board issued its first booklet of modern sequence dances which could be used for competition purposes. This contained 23 dances including 3 Manchester dances - the Cha Cha Margarite arranged by Joe Collier, the Kingston Quickstep and the Red Rose Tango. These were omitted in the next booklet to be published.

Even Walter Whitman of 'Dance News' deplored the fact that a true foxtrot had not been included in the booklet and went on to state that he had never seen a true foxtrot sequence except in formation dancing. There were many true foxtrots at the time but, obviously, not within Walter Whitman's sphere of dancing. This led to the Manchester Area M.C's Club writing a letter to 'Dance News' for possible inclusion in their 'You Tell Us' column. We stated we welcomed the Official Board's recognition of modern sequence but regretted that a true sequence foxtrot had not been included in the booklet and hoped that the Official Board would eventually eliminate those which did not conform to their definition. We also invited any member of the Official Board to attend our next Annual Ball when many modern sequence dances would be seen, including foxtrots. This letter did not get published, however, but mention was made of the Club in a subsequent article by Walter Whitman when he stated that:-

> "views of the Glasgow and District M.C's Association, the Scottish M.C's Association and the Manchester M.C's Club, as well as those individuals with experience of modern sequence, would be helpful at this stage".

However, after all its teething troubles modern sequence has settled down and, with the inclusion of Latin dances, has become one of the cheapest and enjoyable pastimes there is.

It has been impossible to name every dance and arranger and to those arrangers I have missed I tender my apologies as it was not intentional.

Most of the dance originators from those early days have passed on, but some of their sequences are still being danced today and I salute those pioneers of yesteryear.

KEN FULLER

Some Aphorisms!

Dancing adds pleasure to leisure.

Keep fit. Keep young. Keep dancing. Keep it up.

Don't waste music - dance to it.

Don't drink and jive.

Smile when you dance and make it progressive.

SOME USEFUL ADDRESSES

Dance Scripts

1. North Star Publishers, P.O. Box 20, Otley, West Yorkshire, LS21 2SA. 0943 462 269. Publisher of "Sequence Dancing World" (10 issues per year). Supplier of scripts and books of scripts, etc.

2. Brockbank Lane Sequence Script Service, 1a Rodwell Avenue, Weymouth, Dorset, DT4 8UY. 0305 770157. Supplier of scripts (list available) and script accessories. Many scripts have the lady's in addition to the man's steps. Dance records.

3. The Dave Bullen Script Service, 24 Lyndhurst Road, Birkdale, Southport, PR8 4JT. 0704 66922. Scripts, dance records, dancing holidays.

4. Northern Dance Services (NDS), 18-20 Commercial Street, Shipley, West Yorkshire, BD18 3SP. 0274 586829. Large collection of scripts, dance records.

Journals and Newsletters

5. Ballroom Dancing Times, 45/47 Clerkenwell Green, London, EC1R 0BE. 071 250 3006. Monthly. Mainly ballroom but some sequence: usually 2 or 3 scripts per issue.

6. Dance News Ltd., Hamble House, Meadrow, Godalming, Surrey, GU7 3HJ. 0483 428679. Weekly. 16 pages of ballroom dancing news, events, competitions, etc.

Old-Time Dancing

7. The Society for the Preservation and Appreciation of Old-Time Music and Dancing, newsletter.
    Secretary: F. Boast, 8 Bourne Way, Addlestone, Surrey, KT15 2BT, 0932 843475.

Suppliers of Books on Dancing

8. Imperial Society of Teachers of Dancing (ISTD), Euston Hall, Birkenhead Street, London, WC1H 8BE. 071 837 9967.
   Their list includes books on dancing (some on sequence dancing as well as some scripts) and various dancing accessories.

9. Ballroom Dancing Times Book Service, 45-47 Clerkenwell Green, London, EC1R 0BE. 071 250 3006.

Music

(In ordering, make sure that the recordings are designed for sequence with a proper introduction.)

10. Northern Dance Services (NDS), see '4' above.

11. C and D Dance Records, 145 Chestnut Avenue, Eastleigh, Hants., SO5 5BB. 0703 614476.

12. Maestro Records Limited, P.O. Box 85B, East Molesey, Surrey, KT8 9EJ. 081 398 9018.

13. Dancetime Records, P. O. Box 271, Purley, Surrey, CR8 4YL. 081 660 5046.

14. Worldwide Record Distributors Limited, 282 Camden Road, London, NW1 9AB. 071 267 6762.

15. The Dance and Listen Record Co. Ltd., 1 Queens Road, Fleet, Hants., GU13 9LA.

Educational Dance Videos

16. 'Technique on Video', Elizabeth Romain, Grove Cottage, 48 West Street, Ewell, Surrey, KT17 1XB. 081 393 3506.

17. Quasar Video, One Eleven, Hoarwithy, Hereford, HR2 6QH. 0432 840254.

18. Westport (UK) Ltd., Broomhill Road, Brislington Trading Estate, Bristol, Avon, BS4 5RH. 0272 715311.

INDEX OF DANCING FIGURES

159

160

GENERAL INDEX

NOTES